Praise for
The Goals Program

Goals are incredibly powerful. In fact, they can spell the difference between winning and losing in so many areas of life: money, relationships, faith, and careers just to name a few. And no one taught goal-setting better than Zig Ziglar. He was the master, and this book is proof of that.

—Dave Ramsey,
bestselling author and nationally syndicated
radio show host

I've always been a raving fan of Zig Ziglar and I always will be. What I love most about *The Goals Program* is that as I am reading, I can hear Zig's voice urging me to get busy. His trademark enthusiasm and passion leap right off the page into my brain. If you need a jump start on the way to your next goal, there's no better book out there. Thanks, Zig!

—Ken Blanchard,
co-author of *The New One Minute Manager*®
and *Leading at a Higher Level*

For years, I have witnessed the consistent results evidenced in the lives of Zig Ziglar's children. Knowing for a fact that his material was always developed and proven within his own family first, I cannot express how excited I am that *The Goals Program: How To Stay Motivated* is being made available. This book contains the very best from a man who was the very best. The first two copies of *The Goals Program* I purchase will be for my own teenaged boys.

—**Andy Andrews**,
New York Times bestselling author of
The Traveler's Gift and *The Noticer*

Zig Ziglar's 7-step goal setting method is the best of breed. This is a powerful book.

—**Chris Widener,**
New York Times bestselling author

Millions have seen Zig speak, but no one has ever seen this book. Never-before-seen manuscript on Zig's legendary GOALS system is available for the first time in book form.

—**Scott Hogle,**
bestselling author of *PERSUADE*

The wisdom of Zig Ziglar lives on. *The Goals Program: How to Stay Motivated* helps you move from concentrating on the obstacles and difficulties instead of the benefits of taking action to reach your goals. My advice: Get with the program!

—**Harvey Mackay**,
author of the #1 *New York Times* bestseller
Swim With The Sharks Without Being Eaten Alive

This is a classic. Read it five times. Follow the steps and then read it again.

—**Seth Godin**, Founder altMBA

Thanks to Zig Ziglar and the strategies in this book, I've achieved goals beyond what I once imagined were even possible. If you want to learn the simplest and most effective way to achieve goals beyond what you currently believe is possible for you, this is the book that will show you how to do exactly that.

—Hal Elrod,
#1 bestselling author, *The Miracle Morning* and
The Miracle Equation

There are very few books that I will read more than once. Zig Ziglar's *The Goals Program* is going on my annual reading list! If you have ANY desire to improve your goal-setting skill, the time you put into this book will be the best investment you've made.

—Elliott Neff,
Chess4Life CEO and author of *A Pawn's Journey*

WOW. Once again Zig Ziglar proves he is THE MASTER teacher as his new book is FULL of GOLD for the Mind and Heart. He changed my life the first speech I saw him give decades ago and still is changing my life with this new goldmine of a book, *The Goals Program,* for business and life success. Absolute Genius.

—Dr. Doug Firebaugh

The Goals Program

How to Stay Motivated Series
Book 2

Zig Ziglar

Made for Success
PUBLISHING

Made For Success Publishing
P.O. Box 1775 Issaquah, WA 98027
www.MadeForSuccessPublishing.com

Distributed by Made For Success Publishing
Cover Design by Dee Dee Heathman
Interior Design by Dee Dee Heathman

Library of Congress Cataloging-in-Publication data
Ziglar, Zig
     The Goals Program (How to Stay Motivated Book 2)
     p. cm.

    ISBN: 978-1-61339-440-6
    LCCN: 2019953720

       1. Self-Help / Motivational & Inspirational
       2. Business & Economics / Motivational
       3. Religion / Christian Life / Inspirational
       4. Self-Help / Personal Growth / Success

Printed in the United States of America

For further information contact Made for Success Publishing, +1 425 526 6480 or email at service@madeforsuccess.net

Contents

1

YOU AND YOUR GOALS PROGRAM

In 1920, Stanford University embarked on a study of 1,440 genius-level youngsters, following them throughout their lives. When the man who initially did the research retired, they simply passed it on to his associates in the department. Here's what they discovered: Those who became outstanding successes were not successful because of their genius; they were successful because they were able to focus on what was important and *persisted* until they reached it. You don't have to be a genius to do that!

Lots of people have individual goals, but very few have goals *programs*. Several years ago, I was speaking up in the Pacific Northwest, not far from Portland, Oregon. I was presenting to the Northwestern Lumbermen's Association. Now, as my granddaughter would say, this was in the "olden days." You can likely imagine what the lumberjacks looked like—they were big dudes! They all looked like they could have been playing defensive end for the Cowboys.

The man in charge said, "Zig, these people like to hear a lot of stories and jokes, so be sure to keep their attention."

With that in mind, I went off full-speed ahead. After a few minutes, I was interrupted by a great big dude about six feet four, weighing about 275 pounds. He stood up, towering above me, and said, "Zig! I got a story I wanna tell you!"

Now, let me back up for a minute: I have a standard policy. Whenever anybody the size of a linebacker stands up and wants to tell me a story, I let 'em! So I said, "Go ahead, pardner!"

"I wanna tell you about my buddy Bill. Stand up, Bill!" A little dude about five feet two inches tall stood up. In stark comparison to his gigantic friend, Bill couldn't have weighed over 120 pounds soaking wet.

Lumberjack the linebacker continued, "This is my buddy, Bill Carlotta. Now, ol' Bill came into camp here a few weeks ago and walked up to me and said, 'Shake hands with your new tree-topper.' I looked at him and said, 'Bill! A tree-topper! That's a dude that climbs all the way to the top of the tree and cuts the top off, and then you gotta hang on for dear life. That's a job for a man, and you're just a boy!' Ol' Bill didn't do nothin' but pull off his shirt and say, 'I AM a man.' Zig, I'm here to tell you, he is a man. He is all muscle! But I still wasn't convinced. Ol' Bill said, 'Tell you what. Let's go out in the woods. You pick out a tree, tell me how long it would take your best man to put it on the ground, and I'll do it in half the time!'

"Well, we went out in the woods and we picked out this spruce tree, and I don't have a man in camp that could have put it on the ground in less than 40 minutes, but ol' Bill went to work on that sucker and I'll tell you, that ax looked like it was a solid sheet. In less than ten minutes, that tree was on the ground! And I said to him, 'Bill, where on Earth did you learn how to cut down trees like that?'

"He said, 'I learned in the Sahara Forest.'

"'In the Sahara Forest! Bill! The Sahara is a desert!'

"He said, 'It is now!'"

Now, there's a guy who had an attitude that I think you'll agree was an absolutely positive one!

Life is Like a Cafeteria Line

Before we get into the meat of this book, I want to say that life is very much like a cafeteria line. A number of years ago, the Redhead and I saw this new cafeteria. Now, when I talk about my wife, at her suggestion, I always call her The Redhead. When I'm talking to her, it's Sugar Baby. Incidentally, her name is Jean. Anyways. So, this new cafeteria was the Romano's that had just opened out on North Central Expressway. We knew it was going to be good because the line was always out the door! Well, on this particular day we weren't willing to wait that long in line, so we kept going past. Then one day we rode past, and we couldn't see a line, so I said, "Hey! Looks like we can get in there today; let's go!"

We parked, walked in, and quickly understood why the line was not outside. Because it was wound all over the building. We'd already parked, so we got in line, albeit grudgingly. As we got down to the end of the line, we turned around, and there was another line of thirty people. So we were still walking and talking, and we got down to that one, and wouldn't you know it, there was *another* line of thirty people. But this time we could see the food! As we walked down the line, I said to myself, "Now, I'm gonna get me some of that, and I want me some of that. Yeah, that looks good! I'll have me some of that. I want some of that." I love to eat in cafeterias. I like to see what I'm going to eat before I choose it, so I'd already made up my mind.

Now, let me clarify: I don't care how prodigious your appetite is, you cannot eat some of everything that's on the line. When I got to the end of the line, I reached in and took out my money. The lady at the end of the line held up her hand, and she said, "No, you don't pay for it until you get ready to leave."

I said, "You mean you're gonna let me eat all this food before I pay for it?"

She said, "Yeah, that's just the way we do it."

I have since thought about that scenario quite often. Life is exactly like a cafeteria line inasmuch as we've got so many things to choose from. In the Romano's cafeteria line, you get to eat, and then you pay. Now, life is not like that cafeteria line because in life, you pay and then you eat. Your employer will make you work from two to four weeks before he or she will give you a dime. That's the way we treat our people—we make them work before we give them the pay. The farmer plants the crop, raises it, and fertilizes the soil. He does all the things, and then—and only then—can he go to the marketplace and be rewarded for his effort. The students study their lessons. Then they take the test, then they graduate, then they receive the reward. But the point is very simple: You've got to do those things in order for things to happen for you, and this all takes place *before* you're rewarded.

Let's identify what it is that everybody wants. Everyone wants to be happy. They want to be healthy. They want to be at least reasonably prosperous. They want to be secure. They want to have friends. They want to have peace of mind. They want to have good family relationships, and by all means, they want to have hope!

If you want those things, did you specifically identify all of them as goals and write them down? Did you list the benefits of all of those? Now, that's a very important point. A lot of people talk only about the problem. "I'd quit smoking, but I'd gain 38 pounds!" Or, "I'd go back to school and get my degree, but by then, I'll be 45 years old—it'd take me ten years!" Well, all of us have heard the additional thought to that: How old will you be in ten years if you don't go back to school and get your degree? We concentrate on the obstacles and difficulties instead of the benefits.

How many of you are salespeople? If all you talked about was price, how much would you sell? You talk about the benefits that come with it. If you see somebody with braces on their teeth, they're not very happy while they've got them, but the benefits later on are what they really are buying. Did you list the benefits? Do you have the necessary skills and knowledge to reach this objective? Did you identify the obstacles? There are always going to be obstacles in life; we've just got to identify them. Have you identified the individuals, groups, and organizations to work with? Have you developed a plan of action, and have you set the completion date? That's what goal planning is really all about.

Happiness is Now

Now the question comes up, "Well, now, wait a minute, Ziglar! You said everybody wants to be happy. Can you really set *happiness* as a goal?" Well, let's talk about that. All of my life, I've been told you can't set happiness as a goal. Happiness, like money, is the result of what you do. For example, say we're talking about the qualities of success. If you were honest, hard-working, enthusiastic, and had integrity; if you were dependable and responsible, how would you feel about yourself? That image you have of yourself would be a good one. Now, if you are happy with yourself, if you know that you are using the abilities you have, then your chances of being happy dramatically improve.

There are an awful lot of people who will be happy in their own mind when they get the new home. Then they'll be happy when they get everything arranged properly in it, and they'll be happy when they get the new furniture. Then they will be happy when they finish paying for it. Then they'll be happy when they get the patio and the backyard landscaping. It's always a *when* or *where*. "I'll be happy when I win the trip to Hawaii. Then I'll be happy when I get there." No. You will not be happy in a *when* or a *where*.

> **Hapiness is not a *when* or a *where*. It is a here and a *now*.**

What we've got to understand is that you can lose what you have and still be what you are. Now that's very important. Because if you are what you are, if that's what you build on, then the chances of being happy really do increase rather substantially.

How many of you believe that if your health is good, that if you're reasonably prosperous, that if you're secure within your-self and what you do, if you have friends and peace of mind and good family relationships and have hope for the future, your chances of happiness would be improved?

There is no question about it: Peace of mind comes as a result of the resolution of the question of what happens to us when we die. In other words, where do we spend that eternity? That has a direct bearing on the way we live, and there are varying answers to that question. How many of you believe that life is fragile? How many of you have known somebody who was happy one day and miserable the next? If you have an accident, for example, you can be completely healthy one day then tragically injured the next. If your happiness was wrapped up solely in your health, then that happiness goes away.

That's one of the reasons I like to emphasize the point that we need to understand the difference between a problem and a condition. John Foppe is an outstanding young man who was born without any arms; he has a specific condition. If he makes a problem out of it, then he will never be happy because he will never have arms! But if he recognizes it is a condition, then he can learn to deal with the condition. That's actually one of the ways this young man stays so optimistic and motivated and is such a happy person.

A helpful exercise is to take a sheet of paper and draw it in three sections. At the top of one put "BE"; on the middle one put "DO," and on the last one put "HAVE." You will discover that everything you *have* is a result of what you *are* and what you *do*. So that's what we want to work on.

A lot of people think happiness means "I've gotta be ecstatic all of the time." Well, let me tell you something, folks, all sunshine makes a desert. If all you ate was ice cream, you'd get sick and tired of ice cream. What we need to do is understand that a lot of times our greatest trials and tribulations produce the greatest happiness. I've never yet had a mother describe how much fun she had giving birth to a child. But I have had many of them say after the pain was gone, "The ecstasy I felt; the joy and delight, the happiness that came as a result of that, almost immediately made me forget what I said during labor." A lot of mothers say during labor, "This is gonna be the only one of these I will ever have!" But boy, when you hold that little one in your hands, you forget about the trauma that has been involved in the birth itself.

Genuine happiness comes from who you are and what you do with who you are. A lot of people get a lot of pleasure in sinking a 40-foot putt. I was delighted when the Cowboys won the Super Bowl. But do you really think that every Buffalo Bills fan in America is miserable and unhappy just because the Bills lost the Super Bowl? That doesn't mean they didn't want to win, but what it does mean is that it was an event. And their life is not going to be controlled and determined by that particular event. Those people who think they can be happy all the time are simply not dealing with the reality of life.

> **We need to understand that failure is an event; it is not a person. Yesterday really did end last night; today is a brand-new day—and it's yours! You do not need to let what happened yesterday control what you are doing today.**

There are four reasons why 97 percent of all the people in our society do not have a goals program. And that first reason is fear. Now *fear* is an acrostic for "False Evidence Appearing Real." Everybody has goals. But I want to look at a goals program because that is so enormously important. When I say "False Evidence Appearing Real," what do I mean? A young Cuban hijacked a plane to Cuba with a bar of soap. That's all he had. He put the bar of soap in a box, said to the captain, "It's a bomb, let's go to Cuba." So, they went to Cuba. I could literally take a handkerchief and rob a bank or a financial institution. All I'd have to do is put the handkerchief over my face, put my hand in my pocket, make like I had a gun in there and say, "Gimme your money!" The evidence would be false, but it would appear real, and, consequently, the bank would be robbed. I might get shot on the way out, but I would be successful in at least frightening the individual I was dealing with in virtually every case.

A lot of times we are given information about ourselves as youngsters which is absolutely erroneous. We buy into that idea, and we carry that with us, in many cases for the rest of our lives. That's the reason I say we need to understand that failure is an event; it is not a person. Yesterday really did end last night; today is a brand-new day—and it's yours! You do not need to let what happened yesterday control what you are doing today.

Goals and Self-Image

Often when we are thinking about the image we create of ourselves, we accumulate *False Evidence*. For example, it's dangerous to fly airplanes. An example is the near-tragedy that took place at Dallas Fort/Worth Airport. That airplane, as some of you noticed who looked at it, was in pretty bad shape after that landing. It's dangerous to fly. But it's *more* dangerous for the airplane not to fly. Because I'll tell you, when those suckers come down from 30,000 feet up, the trade-in value on them is hardly anything! I mean, you can't swap those dudes in at all! It is more dangerous, however, for the plane to stay on the ground. Experts will tell you that a plane will rust out faster sitting on the runway than it will wear out flying in the heavens. That's because flying is what airplanes are built for.

It's dangerous for a ship to leave the harbor. It might not get back. But it is more dangerous for it to stay in the harbor. Experts say that it will collect barnacles and deteriorate faster riding at anchor than it will sailing the high seas, and that's precisely what ships are built for. It is dangerous for you to set goals. You might not get there. Now you're going to be embarrassed in front of your friends. But it is infinitely more dangerous not to set the goal. It's dangerous for a farmer to plant crops; we all know that. Suppose it rains too much, or not enough. Suppose it gets too cold, or not cold enough. Suppose it's too hot, or not hot enough. It's dangerous to plant those crops. But, I think you'll agree that it is infinitely more dangerous for them not to plant the crops. In other words, it is more dangerous not to set goals than it is to set those goals.

I love the way Harry Emerson Fosdick said it: "No steam or gas ever drives anything until it is combined. No Niagara is ever turned into light and power until it is tunneled. No life ever grows until it is focused, dedicated, and disciplined." I love what Wayne Gretzky, the superstar of hockey said: "It is provable beyond any doubt that you will miss 100 percent of all the shots you never take." There are a lot of people who fail not because they don't have the ability, but because they don't recognize that ability and make the effort to be the success they're capable of being.

Dr. Joyce Brothers says that the picture you have of yourself, your image, determines the job you seek (or profession), the person you marry, the habits you acquire, the way you look and dress, and it even influences your very moral conduct. She says you cannot consistently perform in a manner inconsistent with the way you see yourself.

There are a lot of people who see themselves as $20,000-a-year earners or $30,000-a-year earners or whatever, and once they get there, they can't see beyond that.

The second reason 97 percent of people do not have goals is because of a poor self-image. Change the picture, and you change the performance. Again, you've got to *be* before you can *do*, and you've got to *do* before you can *have*.

In the February 1993 *Teachers In Focus* publication, Duane Crum says this about your conduct concerning your self-image: "The foundation for teens to say 'No' to sex is a healthy self-image." Such an important point. In February of 1992, Educational Communications, Inc., released the results of an HIV/AIDS knowledge and action survey of the high-achieving students listed in *Who's Who Among American High School Students*. Three out of four—that's 75 percent—of the high school seniors said, "We are virgins."

You see, so many people say, "Everybody's doing it!" Well, everybody might be doing it in the media, but not out there in real life. They went ahead to say that it can be summed up in one sentence by those who say no to sex, "I value my own future enough to take steps to protect it." That's self-image, and it's important in every phase of life. The problem of discrimination also dissipates when students believe in themselves. Kids who feel valued are less apt to prove themselves by discriminating against others and may be motivated to assist those who are different. As the California Task Force to Promote Self-Esteem said in *Toward a State of Self-Esteem*, "Persons with healthy self-esteems choose to serve others out of their sense of personal fullness and their joy of being alive. In the process of serving, they deepen and reinforce their own self-esteem. The majority of teens in America are virgins. Every national survey disproves the notion 'everybody' is doing it."

Now, why do I put that information in there so strongly and on a number of different occasions? To prove the point that we can do something about many of our problems, and that simply involves a realistic picture of who we are and what we are capable of doing.

On January 28th, 1978, I was speaking up in Oklahoma City. It was an all-day seminar. About eighteen months later, I got a letter from a man named Tom Hartman. Since then, I have become friends with Tom. I haven't seen him in four or five years, but we had a number of telephone conversations, as well as personal visits. Throughout our correspondence, here was the gist of what Tom Hartman had to say: "Zig, I was there all day. But three minutes after I got there, I knew I was in the wrong place. You came out with a lot of enthusiasm and said, 'You can go where you want to go, you can do what you want to do, you can be like you want to be.' Man, I said to myself I wasn't gonna sit there all day long and listen to that kind of baloney! I mean, I knew better than that! And I just made up my mind that at the first chance I was gonna get out of there! But, you kept goin', and a few minutes later you had the gall to say to that audience, 'God loves you!' I knew that was a bunch of baloney and I immediately wanted to leave, but I was right in the middle of 1,600 people, and knew that I was going to create a disturbance if I did, so I said to myself, 'First break I'm gone, and that'll be the end of me and Zig Ziglar, as far as I'm concerned!' But, Zig, you're such a persistent guy. You kept hammering away! In a few minutes you said, 'You were designed for accomplishment. You were engineered for success. You were endowed with the seeds of greatness.'

"When you said that, I thought to myself, 'Well, the old boy is finally getting closer to the truth!' Because I was lookin' at a 63-1/2" waistline and 406 pounds of bulk. I was just coming off a devastating divorce. I hadn't been in a church in years and years and years. I had a job only because my boss was my friend; the only friend I had. I wasn't workin' because I was productive—I was workin' because, in essence, I was on welfare. He was supporting me. I was so broke that on Friday night I'd go to the grocery store, buy my food, give 'em a hot check, and then Monday morning when I got my check I'd rush over to the bank to beat it.

"I was failing in every area of life. I wasn't happy. I wasn't healthy. I wasn't even reasonably prosperous. I certainly did not feel secure; had only one friend. I had no peace of mind. I had terrible family relationships, and hope? Forget it! In my life, hope didn't exist. But, Zig, you kept hammerin', and I don't know what it was you said, but you mentioned something and some lady behind me said, 'That's right,' or something like that. And you know, at that moment something snapped. It finally penetrated."

Isn't it interesting? A message can go 24,000 miles around the world in less than a tenth of a second, but sometimes it never penetrates that last quarter of an inch. "But," he said, "I reached over and picked up my yellow pad, and I started writing. I wrote fast and furiously all day long. By the end of the day, for the first time in my adult life, I caught just a glimmer of hope. And I wanted so desperately to buy a set of your motivational tapes, but I didn't have a dime to my name. But my brother, bless his heart, he came to the rescue. He loaned me the money, and I bought the tapes. I had listened to you six solid hours that day, but I went home and I listened to you another seven hours.

"When I got up the next morning, I was a totally different human being. I caught a bigger glimpse of what hope was all about. The first thing I did was go to my boss and say to him with a smile on my face, 'Rest easy. I'm gonna start carrying my own weight.' When you weigh 406 pounds, that's a pretty big statement! That afternoon, I went over to Oklahoma City University, and I was already takin' a couple of courses in history there, just to have something to do. I switched 'em over to psychology because I wanted to learn something about me and about my fellow human being.

"That afternoon, I went over to the Nautilus Health Studio to get something done about this miserable body of mine. On Thursday, I went down to the clothing store and laid aside $700 on a minute down payment." He almost grimaced when he said "minute." He said, "The owner of the store, when he noticed I was buying size 47 jackets and size 39 slacks, said, 'Mr. Hartman, who you getting the clothes for?' When I told him I was getting them for myself, he looked very skeptical, but he said, 'OK.' I knew deep down that he didn't believe for a minute that I was going to be able to lose all of that weight."

Taking Action

Now, let me pause just for a moment and look at something. Let's make two points here. The major point is Tom Hartman made the commitment and took action immediately. We discovered that when people first hear this concept of a goals program, if they take action immediately, the chances are at least ten times as high that they'll do something about it. If they delay it; if they say, "Well, I'll get around to it," you know what happens to that one. Second major point: When directions are set and commitments are made, help starts showing up all over the place almost immediately.

Let me tell you what I'm talking about. Tom Hartman said to me in one of our conversations and in one of the letters, "Zig, I since have listened to that tape on self-image over 500 times. I've listened to all of the others a minimum of 200 times. If you ever develop a sore throat, man, don't you dare cancel any speaking engagements. Just call me! I can make your talk verbatim! I'll even use your accent!"

Can you imagine him accusing me of having an accent? "But," he said, "Zig, lemme tell you what happened. I'm so glad that the police did not observe me as I was listening to those tapes. I'd be riding down the street and…" (In those days, they didn't have many tape decks in the automobiles, so he had his cassette player on the seat by him.) He said, "I'd be listening to one of your tapes, and you'd say, 'You were born to win!' and I'd say, 'Well, how come I'm always losing?' And you'd say, 'You can do it!' and I'd say, 'Well, how come I never can or never have?' And you'd say, 'Hang in there!' and I'd say, 'Zig! Hanging is no fun at all!' But you know, Zig, I noticed something. Sometimes I'd get a little weary, and I didn't have as much enthusiasm when I tried to refute you. But you were always motivated! You were always excited! That recording was always wide open, full-speed ahead, no-holds-barred! Over a period of time, I came to realize that what you were saying was absolutely right."

Tom Hartman made a statement that I believe is absolute truth. You know, there is an old saying that truth can be denied, but it cannot be avoided. Ultimately, it would get to you. "Now," he said, "because you were speaking truth, I believe that anybody, regardless of how vehemently they might reject it initially, if they will just hear it enough times, that it will penetrate and get through to them and it will have its impact. I'd been in the program about six weeks when I was in a grocery store buying my food. It was a Friday night. And as I was in that store, there was a little four-year-old girl, and all of a sudden, I heard a screaming voice loud enough that you could have heard it from Dallas to Fort Worth, and she said, 'Mama! Look at that fat man!'" Tom said, "I whirled around to see where he was! Then I realized she was talking about me. I thought that was the funniest thing I'd ever heard in my life. I got so tickled, I literally laughed until I cried. I shed a tear of an entirely different kind because, for the first time in my life, I knew I was gonna make it. I knew that I was gonna take that weight off and change the other things in my life. The picture had changed.

"About a month later, I'd been to the movies. I was on my way back to the car. I was in no hurry. I had nothing to do and nowhere to go; nothing to do when I got there. I was just amblin' along, and I noticed the display in one of the store windows. I had no interest in the display, Zig." We've all done this, but he just walked over and he started looking at the display, and then he became intrigued with it. And suddenly he became aware of the fact that he was not by himself; some big dude was looking over his shoulder. He whirled around. There was nobody there. He had seen his own reflection—which he did not recognize.

Tom Hartman was no longer obese. Though he still weighed well over 360 pounds, he was no longer obese because the picture he had of himself had completely changed.

If you might recall, in my own life, I weighed well over 200 pounds for 24 years. I lost tons of weight. It went up and down and up and down. But 24 years ago, when the picture of myself changed, the weight came off and it is still off. Tom Hartman's picture had changed.

Now, let me emphasize a point. I guarantee that you will discover very quickly that when you start out on a project, there is a conspiracy among people to help you reach your objectives, not to keep you from it. When you know where you're going, the world kind of gets together and says, "Hey! Here's someone who knows where they're going. I want to go with them!" Or, "I want to make it easier for them."

Let me tell you what had happened in Tom Hartman's life. Now, help is sometimes negative, which turns out to be positive. For example, the skeptical store owner where he bought his clothes had said to himself, "I don't think he's going to make it!" Tom Hartman said, "I will show that dude!" The little girl who said, "Look at the fat man!" does not realize how much she helped Tom Hartman to meet his goals. His brother, who bought him those tapes, had certainly been an enormous help to him.

Some of you might say, "But, Zig, didn't I hear you say a few minutes ago that Tom listened to that self-image tape over 500 times?" Yes, that's exactly what I said. "Now, Zig, you gotta be kidding me if you stand there and tell me that he benefitted over 500 times every time he listened to it!" I'm going to make a very strong statement now, a statement which I cannot prove. I honestly believe that more people have lost weight and kept it off as a direct result of listening to my tapes than any diet book that you've ever seen. I know that's a strong statement. But hear me out. I have people, literally by the hundreds who have started conversations with me by saying, "You know, I started listening to those tapes, and I lost 40 pounds!" Or, "I lost 200 pounds," or, "I lost 60 pounds," or whatever. Let me tell you why that happens.

The brain produces some incredible chemicals when activated. Various things activate the brain. For example, exciting music activates the brain; it floods the system with endorphins, dopamine, norepinephrine, and some of the other neurotransmitters.

Exercise and jogging, for instance, will really get them going. Winning a Super Bowl game gets those endorphins hopping and all! Every time Tom listened to the tape, in some cases, it activated the pituitary in the brain. In other cases, other parts of the brain were activated, and his system was flooded with those chemicals, and he was energized physiologically. Dopamine and norepinephrine are your energy chemicals; that's what gets that little get-up-and-go, that little extra step in your life. There's also something in the brain called galanin. Now, galanin is the "bad guy." Dopamine and norepinephrine give you the energy; endorphins give you the endurance, and all of those are produced as we listen to something exciting and motivating.

For the person who is overweight, what happens is the galanin, the "bad guy," literally eats, devours, and destroys the dopamine or the norepinephrine. And so, the more overweight you are, the lower that energy level goes. What Tom Hartman was doing was activating the brain, producing more dopamine, more norepinephrine, more endorphins, and as a result, he developed the energy; he was burning that fat instead of consuming that fat. I believe that is one of the most exciting breakthroughs that I have ever heard or learned in my life! Again, when the picture you have of yourself changes, then everything in your life is going to change.

> **When the picture you have of yourself changes, then everything in your life is going to change.**

"Bought Off" on Goals

The third reason that 97 percent of people do not have a goals program is because they have never been sold. That's my objective now. I'm flat going to sell you on why you've got to have those goals! A program. I'm not going to *try* to sell you; I'm not going to *hope* to sell you. I am flat going to sell you on why you have to have them! As a matter of fact, I'm going to do such a thorough job of it that before you go to bed tonight, you will have taken the first steps in this program. As a matter of fact, I'll make it stronger than that—if you don't take the first steps tonight before you go to bed, you might as well not go to bed, because you're not going to be able to sleep! This is going to be enormously important and exciting.

The typical person in America is what I call a *wandering generality*. They go to work tomorrow because that's what they did yesterday. And if that's the reason for going to work, they're not going to be any better—they might not be as good as they were yesterday because now they're two days older and still have no specific direction in their life. The typical individual, while they're working on their job, gets to thinking, "You know, I ought to be spending more time with my family!" When they're spending time with the family, they're thinking, "I ought to be out there working for my family!" Their mind is in one place while their body is in another, and then they wonder why they're not more effective!

The exciting thing about a goals program is that it enables you to focus so that when you're at home, you're more effective; when you're on the job, you're more effective. This means you will then have extra time for growth, to pursue an education and engage in the activities which will make you more productive in life.

J. C. Penney expressed it enormously well a number of years ago when he said, "Give me a man who is a stock clerk and who has a goal, and I will give you a man who'll make history. Give me a man who is a stock clerk without a goal, and I'll give you a stock clerk." Again, it is not where you are; it's where you go.

One of my favorite stories is about the young man who aspired from his first coaching job at the University of South Carolina. A new head coach had come in and let the old staff go, but he kind of liked this young coach and gave him some fatherly advice. He said, "Son, you're not cut out to be a coach. I encourage you to get into some other field." Well, the young man at that time had a dream. His dream was to be the head football coach at the University of Notre Dame. He thanked the man for his advice, and decided he would continue to pursue his career. At Ohio State University, Woody Hayes gave him a chance. Later, William and Mary made him a head coach; he did such a fabulous job there he got a chance to head coach at North Carolina State University, where he built the best win-loss record that school had ever experienced. He had a short stay—one year in the pros—but learned that he loved to teach young people. He ended up as the head coach at the University of Arkansas, where he built the best win-loss record they'd ever had there as well.

One year, they were invited to the Orange Bowl to play mighty Oklahoma. Three of his players were caught with a woman in the room; he investigated it, verified the fact that it actually had happened, and without any hesitation kicked all three of them off the team. Now, let me emphasize a point: Those three players were the entirety of his offensive team. I mean, 90 percent of the scoring and 90 percent of the yards had been won by those three players. The media speculated that Arkansas should withdraw from the Orange Bowl because they obviously had no chance against Oklahoma. They already were underdogs before he dismissed those three players.

But the coach decided to take stock of what he did have and not worry about what he had lost. So, he analyzed what he had: The number one punter in the entire nation, as well as the number one field-goal kicker in the entire nation. He also had the number one defense in the entire nation, and he had the players identify over and over what their strengths were. The rest, as they say, is history. It almost was a mismatch. They were an inspired football team, and they beat Oklahoma very badly.

Later he went to the University of Minnesota, which at one time had a tremendous football program and a winning season. When he signed the agreement with them, he asked for two escape clauses. In his own words: "Number one, if the powers that be at Notre Dame say to me 'We want you to coach the team,' and if I have had you in a Bowl within three years, I want to be released from my agreement." They agreed to it. Well, at the end of the second year, Notre Dame University called Lou Holtz to be their head football coach. Goals absolutely do work.

But let me emphasize something very significant. They called him to be the coach the day he dismissed those three players from his Arkansas football team. They said, "Here's the man who is more interested in developing character and developing people for life; not just winning football games." The powers that be said, "If he's ever available at the time we need a coach, he is our man."

Goals, built on a solid base, absolutely do work.

David Jensen of UCLA, the chief administrative officer for the Crump Institute, the UCLA School of Medicine, did a study on the people who come to this seminar, set goals programs, and develop that plan of action that we're going to be talking about to follow through on the goals program. In this study, here's what he learned: Those who set their goals and developed a plan of action earned an average of $7,401 a month. Those who had exactly the same information but thought it was, "Nice, just not for me! Maybe later, but not now," earned an average of $3,397 a month. It pays to set goals. Literally.

But you know what's even more exciting in that study? Number one was the fact that their family life improved. Number two, their health also improved. Number three, their life balance was infinitely better. That's what a goals program is all about. You have to have them. Can you imagine Sir Edmund Hillary, the first man to scale Mt. Everest, the tallest mountain in the whole world, climbing down off that mountain and some reporter comes to him and says, "Tell me, Sir Edmund! How'd you climb the tallest mountain in the whole world? How'd you do it?" You think for one moment he said, "Well, I was just out there walking around..."? Isn't that ridiculous?

Yet, aren't there an amazing number of people who will spend more time planning the wedding than they will the marriage? Who will spend more time planning a two-week vacation than they will their very life itself? Sir Edmund Hillary did not scale Mt. Everest the first time he tried. As a matter of fact, he left several of his climbers dead on the mountainside. But the effort was so enormous that the British Parliament called him before them to give him England's highest award, and as he walked into that august body as an individual, they rose and gave him a prolonged standing ovation. There was a huge picture in front of the peak of Mt. Everest. He ignored the crowd, walked straight to the front of that picture, and literally shook his fist at it. He said, "You won—this time! But you're as big as you're ever going to get! I'm still growing."

If you didn't reach your goals the first time you set them … so what? Again, I say to you, failure is an event; it is not a person. Yesterday ended last night. Today is a brand-new day. The obstacles might still be there, but when you continue to grow, your chances of scaling that obstacle and reaching your goal are rather dramatically improved.

I don't know how many of you recognize the name Howard Hill. A good Alabama boy, he entered 283 archery tournaments in his lifetime. He placed first 283 times. He killed a Cape buffalo and a Bengal tiger with just a bow and arrow. I have seen him in newsreels from fifty feet away literally split the bull's eye dead center, and then with his next arrow, split the first one! He was remarkable in his skill. They say he could outshoot any rifleman in the world from fifty feet. He killed a fifteen-foot shark in eighteen feet of water—or was it an eighteen-foot shark in fifteen feet of water? Well, all I know, it was a great big'un, and it was way down there!

Now, when I make this statement, I know many of you are going to raise your eyebrows. I've never shot the bow and arrow professionally, but I am an absolutely superb instructor. As a matter of fact, casting modesty aside, I'm going to tell you without any fear of error that I can take any one of you and, if your health is good and your eyesight is good, I could spend twenty minutes with you and have you hitting the bull's eye more consistently than Howard Hill could have hit it the best day he ever had! Provided, of course, we had first blindfolded Howard Hill … and turned him around a few times, so he'd have no earthly idea which direction he was heading. Of course, you understand with a kind of laugh, and you say, "Why, Ziglar, that's the silliest example I have ever heard in my life! How on earth could a man possibly hit a target he could not even see?" That's a good question.

Here's one that's even better. How can you hit a target you don't even have? Do you have one? Let me tell you what our objective is in all of this. I want to help you move from survival to stability, from stability to success, and from success to significance.

As far as these goals are concerned, did you write them down?

Did you identify the benefits which would come your way by reaching them?

Did you spell out the obstacles you've got to climb in order to get there?

Did you identify the people, the groups, and the organizations you need to work with in order to get there?

Did you develop a plan of action?

Did you identify what you need to know?

Have you set a date on when you will get there?

That's what I am talking about when I really get into the goals program.

Now, a lot of times people say, "OK, Ziglar, the first reason I don't have goals is because of fear. The second reason I don't have goals is because of my poor self-image. The third reason I don't have goals is simply because I've never been totally convinced that

I have to have them, and the fourth reason that I do not have goals is because I don't know how."

That, ladies and gentlemen, is going to be the second chapter in this book. Exactly how do you set those goals?

2

THE SPECIFICS OF
SETTING GOALS

The fourth reason 97 percent of people don't have goals is that they really do not know how to put together a goals program. Personally, I think everybody ought to write a book. I'll tell you what the title of the book ought to be: *What You Ought to Do to Get the Most Out of Life.* When I wrote *See You at the Top*, I could have used that as the title because that was really what I was saying. What do you do to get the most out of life on a permanent basis?

The first words I wrote in this book were the words I used in the Tom Hartman story earlier: You can go where you want to go, you can do what you want to do, and you can be how you want to be. Those are no longer the first words in the book, but that's what I had originally written. As I wrote those words, I looked at them and started talking to myself. Talking to yourself is OK, you know. But when I wrote those words, I noticed I was holding the book way out there! The reason was because I had a 41-inch waistline. Over 200 pounds of Ziglar stood between me and the book. The thought occurred to me that one day one of you folks who read this book would come up to me and you would have said, "Ziglar, you believe all that stuff you write?"

I was going to say, "Of course I do!"

Then I could imagine you saying, "Do you believe it all?"

I'd say, "Why, certainly I do!"

Then I can imagine you literally poking your finger in that 41-inch waistline and saying, "Ziglar, do you really believe it all?"

Then I was going to have to say, "Well, you know, us authors, we do take a little literary license every once in a while."

"In other words, Ziglar, you lied about it!"

"Hey, friend, don't call me a liar! People don't like liars!"

"Well, you're at least a hypocrite!"

"Man, don't call me a hypocrite! People sure don't like hypocrites!"

I knew that if I was going to put those words in that book, I had to do something about me. So I went down to the Cooper Clinic where they put me on a diet and exercise program. Dr. Randy Martin was the examining physician, one of those highly motivated, dedicated, committed, dyed-in-the-wool, real health enthusiasts. He was slender and was signed up to run in the Boston Marathon. The first thing they did was take two quarts of my blood. Well, it looked like two quarts. They filled so many vials I thought they were taking a collection for the blood bank!

Then they put me on the treadmill, and on the treadmill the idea is you walk and you walk and you walk and you walk, and the longer you can walk, the better your physical condition is. Well, I looked at that needle and the worst possible condition was "Horrible." I determined to get out of that into just "Awful," and I made it by about four seconds. When it was all over, Dr. Martin called me in for the consultation, and he said, "Mr. Ziglar, you're gonna be delighted to know that you, sir, are not overweight!"

I said, "That is wonderful!"

"However, I need to tell you that you are exactly five and one-half inches too short!"

"Well, Doc, what can I do about it?" He proceeded to give me a sheaf of paper that was thicker than the book itself. By the time he got through telling me what I could do, he'd told me a whole lot more than I really wanted to know.

He ended up by saying, "Mr. Ziglar, I just want you to know that you are in marvelous physical condition."

I said, "Well, that's marvelous!"

"For a 66-year-old!"

"Doc! I'm 46!"

"You are in awful shape!"

I'm telling you, it's your perspective there! So again, he went through all of the things I could do. When I got home, the Redhead said, "Well, I suppose you're going be out running all over the neighborhood."

"Yes, I am."

"Well," she said, "if I'm gonna have a 46-year-old fat boy running all over the neighborhood, I'm gonna get you lookin' as good as I can." So, she went down and bought me some fancy running shirts and shorts. I'd already gotten the shoes the doctor had recommended. Then I did something that was very, very ugly. However, I had not read Ann Landers at the time, and I'll use that as my excuse. Ann Landers said you should not steal pages out of other folks' magazines. Now, there was a magazine in Dr. Cooper's office. It was an old magazine. It had an advertisement in there for Jockey shorts. I don't know if you used to read the Jockey shorts ads or not, but if you didn't, you can probably look them up online and at least look at the picture. First thing you'll discover is they didn't put Jockey shorts on fat boys! Well, at the very least, they didn't have a "Goodyear." I took that picture, I hung it up on my bathroom mirror, and I said, "Now, that's my hero. That's the way I'm gonna look right there!"

The next morning, that opportunity clock sounded off at 5:30. I rolled out of bed, put that fancy running outfit on, hit the front door and I ran a block. But I did better the next day! I ran a block and a mailbox. The next day it was a block and two mailboxes, and then a block and three, a block and four, and a block and five. I well remember the day I ran all the way around one block. I woke the whole family up and said, "Guess what Dad has done?" One day I ran a half a mile, then a mile, then two, then three, then four, then five. I started doing sit-ups; I was only able to do eight the first time. Then I could do ten, then twenty, then thirty, then fifty, then a hundred, then two hundred. I started doing pushups. I could only do six the first time; then I could do eight, then ten, then twenty, then thirty, then forty. Later I was able to do the "GI" pushup, which simply means you push up, and while you're in the air, you slap your hands. Then I advanced to finger pushups.

My weight started coming down from 202 to 165. Incidentally, if you are really interested in losing weight, there are four things you need to do: Step one, and by far the most important: stay away from cottage cheese. Step two: Get a thorough physical examination. Number three: Make certain you see a skinny doctor. A fat doctor cannot tell you how to lose weight! He or she obviously does not believe it's important, or they would have done something themselves. Step four, make certain you get yourself a positive doctor. What's a positive doctor? Most doctors, when they start talking to you about weight, say "Don't eat this, don't eat that, leave that alone, and don't touch that!" I mean, if you like it, you can't have it; if you don't like it, eat all you want!

I love Dr. Martin's approach to eating proper food. He said, "Mr. Ziglar, you're going be delighted to know that you can eat anything you want! As a matter of fact, I have made you a list of what you are going to want!"

Now, there are a lot of different diets, a lot of different diet books. I just happen to believe Dr. Cooper's book, *The Aerobics Program to Total Fitness* is a positively marvelous book on that particular subject.

The reason I give you the particular details on losing that weight and writing a book to lose 37 pounds—if you need to lose any weight, obviously—is simply because it gives you the example that we can follow all the way through in setting those goals. A goal properly set is at least partially reached.

A goal properly set is at least partially reached.

A Successful Goals Program Takes Time

What is the step-by-step process? Let me give you the bad news first. It takes time to do this. In order to do this properly, to have a complete, well-balanced goals program, it will take you somewhere between ten and twenty hours. Now that's a lot of time. That discourages a whole lot of people. But I can absolutely guarantee you that if you follow this procedure, you will save anywhere from two to as many as ten hours every week, which will enable you to do the things which not only are important but are significant. Things you really want to do.

You will start realizing that time is your greatest asset, and the use of that time plays a major role in what you're able to get done in life. So, remember: The bad news? It takes time to set them. Good news? It does save you a lot of time.

Here's some more good news: If you can figure out what twelve times twelve is, you can also figure out what 2,865 times 9,412 is. The reason you can do that is there is a precise formula you follow. When you learn how to set a physical goal, you also will know how to set a mental, spiritual, social, financial, or family goal, because the procedure is exactly the same. There is no mystery to it. It is simply a procedure.

Step one: In order to set your goals, you need to take a sheet of paper. You need to PRINT everything you want to be or do or have. Now a lot of people say, "Well, now, Ziglar, that'll take me three days!" I can assure you that fully 90 percent of everything you want to be or do or have that's in your mind at this point will be on paper within an hour. Print everything.

Why do we say print it? Printing requires more concentration. That burns it more deeply into the subconscious mind. If you program your left brain, that releases your creative right brain. If you follow these steps, I can absolutely assure you it will catapult you many, many steps forward.

In the September-October 1992 issue of *Psychology Today*, there was a fascinating article in there about why Chinese math students do so much better than American math students. You know what they gave as the prime reason? The Chinese students learn their multiplication tables until it almost becomes nauseating. They drill them over and over and over and over again. That left brain is completely programmed. You wake one of them up at 2:30 in the morning and say, "What is 23 times 31?" and BANG! They can give you the answer. What they have done is simply program the brain so carefully that when they get into the abstract, which requires that creativity, they're infinitely more effective.

Think about this: How many times have you ever heard a coach talking about one of his players when the media is asking a question, and he says, "Well, you just can't coach that!" Michael Jordan, I believe, is one of the greatest athletes to ever live, but Jordan has such tremendous athletic skills and incredible amounts of creativity. Let me tell you why he's so creative. He has spent thousands of hours learning all the fundamentals—the dribble, the pass, the over-the-shoulder, the anticipation—and when he gets in a situation he's never been confronted with before (there has never been a game where every player is not confronted with something he's never been confronted with before), he then has such a fundamentally sound left brain that he is free to use his creative right brain. Now, fortunately, he has the athletic skills to follow through on that creativity.

One of the mistakes that industry is learning right now is simply this: You can get promoted too fast. You can move up too quickly. You can move up before you have all of the details so fundamentally sound in your left brain that your creativity is never really freed to come up with innovative new ideas in doing the job you are doing. One of the reasons top management has to go to the bottom rung to ask questions about ways to improve is because that individual has been doing that routine job thousands of times, and in the process, they've come up with some creative ideas. But because of their personality and positions, and because of the *closed-door policy* that a lot of businesses have, they do not want to go to the upper levels and say, "I've got an idea!" When you print it, then you're really disciplining your left brain, you're learning it thoroughly, which frees the right brain.

Step two is to wait from 24 to 48 hours. Personally, I'm convinced that 48 hours is better. In the 48-hour period, keep the list with you because you will add six or eight, ten or twelve other things to that goal list. Then, at the end of the 48 hours, after each thing you printed, ask yourself the question "why?" do I want to be? Or do? Or have? If you can't answer in one sentence why you want to be or do or have, then at this time that really is not a viable goal for you to work on.

Let me tell you why I told the cafeteria story. The cafeteria story made the point that you can't eat everything on the cafeteria line. In life, you can't have everything that is out there. In America, there are over 50,000 ways to earn a living. You'd starve to death if you tried to do 50,000 things to earn a living. You have to get focused. Our main objective is to shorten that list. You can't be, do, and have everything. For example, you can't spend quality time with the family and be the president of the service club and the PTA; be rude and nasty and have friends; be a spendthrift and accumulate wealth; eat Braum's French Chocolate ice cream three times a day and be physically fit.

You can't work all day and party all night. You can't golf or fish five days a week, spend three hours watching TV daily and get your Master's Degree. You can't write a daily column and play on the company softball team; you can't attend all plays, games, and church socials. You can't do all of these things.

Let me tell you about a little game I play. About every three years, I start a list of things I would like to do. The purpose of doing this is so that we can learn to say no to the good so we can say yes to the best. That's part of maturity. That's part of responsibility. That's part of making decisions and the right choices. Last time I did this, I started listing all the things I would like to do that year. Here are some of them:

- ✓ Conduct more family seminars
- ✓ Start a daily radio program
- ✓ Write a daily newspaper column
- ✓ Campaign to get a lot of the advertising of booze, violence, and sex off television
- ✓ Work in the political campaigns to get qualified people in public office
- ✓ Spend more time with my staff
- ✓ Write at least one book a year
- ✓ Learn how to speak Spanish
- ✓ Become more socially involved with my neighbors
- ✓ Read and research a minimum of three (preferably four) hours each day
- ✓ Spend an hour getting in good physical condition
- ✓ Be more active in the civic and social clubs
- ✓ Set a record for those people my age on the treadmill over at the Cooper Clinic
- ✓ Go to Russia and China
- ✓ Play golf five days a week
- ✓ And a number of other things

When I put all of those things together and guesstimated the amount of time it would take to do it, it came up to 368 hours a week. Now, folks, there are only 168 hours in the week. So, what have I got to do? I have got to start eliminating the things that are not really important in my life. Until I put it down, I might have been guilty of saying, "I wanna do this and I wanna do this and that and the other…" That's the reason so many people go through life frustrated.

One of the things that concerns me about much of our advertising is the promise they give you in sixty seconds that if you will use this deodorant or use this shaving cream, or if you will use this perfume, that you will be irresistible to members of the opposite sex. That if you will do this, you'll go right to the top! That is an illusion. But if you repeat it often enough, it becomes believable. Let me say that unrealistic expectations are the very seedbed of depression. What we're trying to do here is get a program in place, so we'll know what we really want to do in life and plan it so that we have a legitimate chance of making it.

Psychology Today says that a 20-year-old American has ten times as good a chance of being depressed as did his 40-year-old father, and 20 times as good a chance of being depressed as did his 60-year-old grandfather. Why is that? Unrealistic expectation is what I'm talking about. We need to have a reason for believing we can do certain things.

Build Confidence for Big Ideas

One of the things that we really want to emphasize here is that we need to have some basic understanding about our goals themselves. For example, some goals must be big. It's the big goal that creates that excitement.

I love the story of old Gentleman Jim Corbett. The heavyweight champion of the world was out doing his roadwork one morning, and he saw a fisherman having a field day. He was pulling little ones and pulling big ones, fast as he could cast he was pulling a fish! But Corbett noticed that he was throwing back the big fish and he was keeping the little ones. He'd never seen that done before. He ran over to the fisherman, and he said, "Man, I love to fish myself! You're doing something I've never seen done before. You're throwing the big ones back and keeping those little ones! Why on earth are you doing it?"

The fisherman sadly shook his head and said, "Man, you don't know how badly I hate to do this, but I just flat don't have a choice. You see, all I've got is just this little ol' bitty frying pan!"

Now before we laugh too loudly, let me emphasize a point. He's talking about you, and he's talking about me. So many times we get the big dream, the big goal, the big idea. No sooner do we get it than we say, "Oh, no, Lord! Don't give me such a big one! All I've got is just this little ol' bitty fryin' pan! Gimme a small one! Oh, no! Besides, you know that's not a good idea! If it were any good somebody else would have thought about it a long time ago!"

Isn't it tragic that we have such little confidence in ourselves? Again, that's the purpose of this book: Build the confidence. Then when those big ideas hit you, you start working on how you engineer them in such a way that you can get it done. You've got to have some big goals.

You've also got to have some long-range goals. On Monday afternoon, I get on board an aircraft headed for Miami, Florida. Twenty minutes later, it will not be going to Miami because the direction and velocity of the wind will change. The gravitational pull of the earth, the moon, the sun, and the stars will pull it slightly off course, so the captain of the aircraft will turn it around, come back to Dallas / Fort Worth airport, land and then we'll start over.

What is the captain of the aircraft going to do? He is not going to change his decision to go; he is going to change his direction to get there. You'd be amazed at the number of people who set an objective, encounter an obstacle, then immediately throw up their hands and say, "Well, I guess I'm not supposed to do it!" Instead of being creative and changing directions to get there, they abandon the goal itself.

Let me tell you why you've got to have long-range goals: They help you to overcome short-range frustrations. Now, I'm not going to be negative. I'd be like that little boy who came home from school one day and said, "Dad, I'm afraid I flunked that arithmetic test."

His dad said, "Son, that's negative! Be positive!"

He said, "Dad, I'm positive I flunked that arithmetic test!"

I'm positive when I say this: You've got trouble, disappointments, defeats, reversals, and setbacks in your life. You think your kid's going to be the starting quarterback; he's not gonna make the cut. You think you're going to make the big sale; you lose the last one you made. You think you're going to get the promotion; you're fired. You think everything is lovely, only to discover that everything isn't lovely! That is part of life. If you've got a long-range goal program that is balanced, when those things happen, you will regard them as a pebble on the beach (depending, of course, on the severity). But many times, it is *the* pebble on the beach. If you don't have real direction in your life and for your life, then you think it's the whole oceanfront.

> **Go as far as you can see, and when you get there you'll be able to see further.**

The rule is this: You go as far as you can see, and when you get there, you'll be able to see further.

The Goals Program

Some goals must be small, and they must be daily. Now, that's the boring part. It also is the most exciting part! However, it requires discipline. Every time you take a step forward, you realize that you are making progress. As the old sayings go: "You can eat an elephant one bite at a time" and "By the mile, it's a trial; by the inch, it's a cinch."

Some goals must be ongoing. What do I mean by *ongoing*? For example, educational goals must be ongoing. An amazing number of people think when they get their diploma or degree, their educational days are over. In actuality, that's when your education really begins. Building a healthy self-image is an ongoing goal. You can have a marvelous self-image today; disaster strikes tomorrow, and then you say, "I am a nothing! I am a nobody!" What we've got to do is have ongoing goals. Building a better relationship with my mate and my children is an ongoing goal. Getting better at my job is an ongoing goal.

Some goals could require consultation. The Redhead and I have a financial consultant. You might ask: "Well, Ziglar, don't you know how to manage the money?" No. Not as well as the finance expert does! So I need somebody to consult with who has that expertise.

When I went to see Dr. Martin, I knew I needed to lose weight. That was obvious! I just didn't know how much. He said, "Here is how much you need to lose." We were able to focus because it was specific and it involved small daily objectives.

Now, I have a consultant I always go to when I have some things I want to get done, particularly if they are very important. I do a lot of praying over it and ask God, "Is this the goal for me?" A lot of times, people say, "Well, what does God say?" I assure you He doesn't always say, "Yeah, Zig, go do that!" But I can tell you this: If it is not the right goal for me, He will not give me any peace about working toward it. Anyway. Get a consultant; that's what I'm talking about.

A number of years ago, I was aboard an aircraft flying over Niagara Falls. We were at about 30,000 feet. The captain of the aircraft said, "Those of you who are seated on the right-hand side of the aircraft, I'm going to tilt the plane slightly left. You should take a look at Niagara Falls." Well, the plane was about half empty, so I went to the left. Now, 30,000 feet is roughly six miles up in the air. That's a long way off. But even from six miles' distance, the enormous power of 180 million gallons of water a minute flowing over those falls is amazing! That's an enormous amount of water! The spray was coming up, and even at 30,000 feet, you could see it clearly! You would be impressed with the awesome power of Niagara Falls. Yet, for years and years and years, that awesome power fell to the rocks below and dissipated into the distance.

> **When we focus our lives, we unleash an incredible amount of power in our lives.**

Then, one day a man came along and said, "You know, I wonder what would happen if we did some construction here and took a small portion of that power, focused it on a specific point, got it to turn some wheels and generate some hydroelectricity?" Bottom line is they have farmed millions of acres of ground, created thousands of jobs, educated children, and built homes, schools, and hospitals because of that idea. They've prospered simply because that power is focused. When we focus our lives, then we unleash an incredible amount of power in our lives.

Set a Goal, Ask a Question

Next, you need to check for balance in areas of your life. What's the purpose of all of these steps? Every step is designed to let you mark off some of the things you've previously written down. You just can't successfully have a hundred goals and work on them all at the same time. Check all of the things that remain for balance—physical, mental, spiritual, personal, family, career, social, and financial. You might go down the list and ask yourself a question:

- *If I reach every one of these goals, will I be happy, healthy, reasonably prosperous, secure, have friends, peace of mind, good family relationships, and hope in the future?* Or do I have it skewed in one or two areas? Too much physical? Too much financial? Not enough social? Not enough family? Ask yourself the question, *Do I have a balanced goals program?*

- *Is this really my goal?* Do I really want to drive a new Lincoln (or a Lexus, or whatever)? Is that what I really want? Or do I want to get one because "that sucker down the street's got one, and if that dude can get one, I can get me one, too!" Do I want to go to this university because it's the best university for me to get exactly what I want to further my career, or do I want to go there because a good friend of mine is going, and we want to go to the same school? You need to ask yourself the question, *Is this really my goal?*
We've got a lot of preachers, plumbers, lawyers, doctors, and CPAs ... and a whole mess of other people who are not nearly as good as they could be because they're not doing what they really wanted to do. Their parents,

grandparents, preachers, or professors had said, "You oughta be this!" Then, without really giving it any further thought, somebody else set their goal. *Is this really my goal?*

- *Is it morally right and fair to everyone concerned?* You cannot be permanently happy at somebody else's expense. Nor can you be permanently happy if it violates the moral and ethical principles upon which society itself must rest. As an aside, any society where "everything goes," eventually is going to be gone.

- *Will reaching this goal bring me closer to or further from my major objective in life?* As an example, if you're having financial difficulties, take questions number two and three and write them on a three-by-five card. Put them in your pocket or wallet, and every time you are tempted to take your credit cards out, then that's the first thing you see. Ask those questions: Is it morally right, and will reaching this goal bring me closer to or further from my major objective in life?

A young man whom I'm very close to and love very much came to me many years ago when CDs and CD players first came out. He said, "Zig, can you get me a discount on a CD player?"

"Well, probably so."

"I'd sure like to get one of those things."

Now, let me say I was privy to a lot of information about this young man. He loves electronic gadgets, and if it has anything to do with music, man! If it's available, it's got to be his! So I said, "Well, now, let me ask you a question before we go buy it."

He said, "OK."

"Is it morally right and fair to everyone concerned?"

He thought about that for a moment and said, "Yeah, I think it's morally right and fair to everyone concerned."

"OK. Next question. Will getting this CD player take you closer to or further from your major objective in life?"

He looked at me and replied, "You just don't want me to have it!"

I said, "No. Hey! It's your deal!"

But let me say again, I was privy to some special information. The young man was a carpenter. His objective was to move up in the construction business. He wanted to be a subcontractor. In order to be a subcontractor, you've got to have a lot of tools. He didn't have those tools. He didn't need to spend that money on a CD player—if he was truly working toward his goals, he needed to be buying tools.

Now, I'm not going to tell you those two questions are the reason why all of the following things happened, but I am going to be bold enough to say they played a part. Number one, he did not get the CD player. Number two, today he's a superintendent with one of the three largest home builders in America, and in his state last year the homes he was in charge of represented 62 percent of all of the homes they built.

When you begin to focus on what is important, when you ask those tough questions and then answer them, that's when things happen in your life.

- *Can I emotionally commit myself and finish this project?* That is an enormously important question, so answer it honestly and sincerely.

- *Can I see myself reaching this goal?* Do I have a visual picture of myself getting there? When you answer that question, then things begin to happen.

Negative Goals, Give-Up Goals, and Go-Up Goals

Check for the negativity in your goal. When I say "check for negativity," what do I mean? Well, you see, goals need to be big. They need to be out of reach, but it's important that they not be out of sight. Because if they're out of sight, you quickly realize you can't get there, you grow discouraged, and then you abandon the whole idea.

I was conducting a seminar in Detroit a number of years ago. A $2,500 sales investment was required for people to get in that franchise operation. A young man who had previously asked me a question did not have the $2,500. He came up to me after a goals seminar and said, "Man! I'm so excited! You have made me a million dollars! That's my goal for this year!"

I said, "Well, now, I hope you will share it with me, then!"

He got a little irritated because he felt I was making fun of the goal. He said, "Well, you don't believe I'm going to do it, do you'?"

Now I was faced with a very important ethical question: Do I exercise positive thinking and say, "Man, you can do it!" or do I really look at the facts and counsel him on maybe changing that objective? Well, here are the facts: He was 25 years old; he'd been working seven years, and he'd been unable to save $2,500 in seven years. Now, folks, that's less than $400 a year. That year, his plan was to make a *million dollars*? First, he had to raise the $2,500 to buy the franchise. Call me blunt, but that was totally unrealistic!

I said, "Well, I tell you what we'll do. Let's see if we can't break this down and determine whether or not that is a realistic goal." That's the process we're going through right now.

I had another young man whom I will never forget come to me, and he said, "Man, my goal is I'm going to be the light heavyweight boxing champion of the world." Well, here was a guy of 31 years old. He weighed about 30 pounds too much for his height. I asked him, "Well, how much experience have you had?"

He said, "Well, I've never been in the ring, but my brother-in-law and I were out sparring the other day, and you can't believe how easily I handled him!"

You see, that young man would've gotten killed by even a fair amateur. We had to talk about a different goal, like losing weight; getting in superb physical condition, and then look at an additional goal. They're negative goals if they are too big. They're negative goals if they're out of your field of study and basic interests. Also, your goal can be negative if you believe that luck is going to have to be the determining factor in reaching that goal.

Now, as an aside, I've frequently been asked the question, "Who do you share your goals with?" Here is a basic answer to that question: If it is a *give-up goal*, tell everybody! What's a *give-up goal?* You know it's a give-up goal when you find an enormous amount of support and encouragement when you share that goal. Everybody will say, "Man, that is great! You can do it!" That's what the 12-Step Programs are all based on. You go to those programs and you hear other people say, "I did it! You can too! Here's how." All of it is tied together. You share those give-up goals with everybody. That strengthens your commitment. It strengthens your resolve, and the chances of reaching it go up exponentially.

Now you share your *go-up goals* very carefully. What's a *go-up goal?* "I'm going to be the starting quarterback." "I'm going to write the best-selling novel." "I'm going to write the greatest self-help book ever!" You go around telling everybody that, you're a salesperson.

Let's say we've got two salespeople down here, this man and this lady, and one of them says to the other, "I'm going to be the number one salesman in the company this year!" The other says to herself, "In a pig's eye, you are! I'm going to be the number one salesperson in the company!" Well, who should you tell that goal? Both of them should go to the sales manager and say, "Help me devise a plan so I could be the number one salesperson." The sales manager will encourage you. Ideally, your mate will encourage you. Share your goals with people you know are going to give you the encouragement you need in order to get there.

Work the remaining goals through the process. Whether the goal is to raise positive kids, get a better education, buy a new car, become the number one salesperson, lose 37 pounds, get a significant raise, acquire a new home, be a better mate or parent, or build a healthy self-image, you need to work them through the process.

The 5-Step Goal-Setting Process

Now, what is the goal-setting process?

1. Identify your goal and write it down.

For example, my original goal was to weigh 165 pounds and have a 34-inch waistline. That's what I committed to writing.

2. List your benefits for reaching that goal.

More energy. This is what everybody was saying, and what all of the books were saying as well. *Less illness.* For example, the first sixteen years after I got on this program, I missed one day of work because of illness. Sixteen years! (That does not include the time my gallbladder ruptured.) I would look and feel better. The Redhead says I look better since I lost that weight. *Longer life span*. All the statistics show that. *Better endurance*. That certainly proved to be true! *More productivity. Better attitude and disposition. More creativity*. Absolutely unbelievable! "Better example to others." I listed my benefits. This is why I want to lose that weight, or get a better job, or buy the new house, or get a better education, or raise positive kids—it doesn't make any difference what it is, you must go through the process.

3. Identify the major obstacles and mountains to climb to reach this goal.

Well, I have a tremendous love for sweets. I can literally eat sweets three times a day, seven days a week, 365 days a year. You know, it's amazing how we come up with a lot of excuses. Bad weather is one of them. I have jogged when it was forty degrees below zero. I've jogged when it was 115 out there. I've jogged when it was sleeting and snowing and a pouring-down rainstorm. Where was I jogging? I was either jogging in my room in place, or I was running up and down the corridor, or I was in a parking garage running. I would find a place to run. I have jogged in Alaska. I've jogged in London, England, right across the street from Buckingham Palace. I've jogged in South Africa on safari—as a matter of fact, I jogged faster there than I've ever jogged in my life! I've jogged in a vast number of places. The point I want to make is when you make the commitment and you realize what the benefits are, then you're going to look at those things and you look at the problem and you explore the solution.

My schedule is incredibly irregular. Can I jog at the same time every day? No way! But you know, I've noticed something. I've never had anybody say to me, "Zig, when on earth can I find time to eat? I mean, this is a problem with me! I am so busy I never have time to eat!" You do what you schedule to do, and you schedule what is important.

I had terrible eating habits, I really did. Especially eating fried foods, eating late at night, and sweets. I was in really poor physical condition. You know, when you're in bad shape, you don't have the energy to go out there and get in shape! But I discovered an astonishing thing. Before I started jogging, I would finish a seminar utterly exhausted. Once I started jogging, it would activate the pituitary gland, flood my system with endorphins (nature's painkiller, incidentally), and my endurance would increase. Now, what's the bottom line? I didn't have time *not* to jog. The reason I say that is because for every 30 minutes I ran, it gave me an additional two hours of high-voltage productivity. It's an investment; it is not *spending* time.

> **Do the things you *want* to do and discipline yourself to do the things you *need* to do.**

I also had a lack of discipline. Boy, that was the tough one for me. But when you discipline yourself to do the things you *need* to do, the days are going to come when you can do those things you *want* to do; and you will be able to do them when you want to do them.

4. Identify what skill or knowledge is required to reach this goal.

Well, I only needed to know two things here, about exercise and jogging and the diet. That's where the Cooper Clinic came in handy for me.

5. Who are the individuals, groups, companies, and organizations to work with?

Well, again, I worked with Dr. Ken Cooper and Dr. Randy Martin, and obviously, the Redhead and I had to agree on when was the best time. Sometimes I would come in at six o'clock, and she would say, "Honey, I am so hungry. Can we eat now?" Well, I wanted to run! Now, what did we do? I went ahead and did the dinner with the Redhead and then a couple of hours later that evening is when I ran. You've got to keep everything in balance.

I have one friend who gets up every morning at five o'clock and runs for an hour. Bottom line, he never has any time in the morning to spend with his family. You've got to fit it in so you don't alienate the people who are important to you. That's the reason for the complete goals program itself.

Now, why do I need to work with my secretary? That ought to be very, very obvious. When we schedule a speaking engagement, I frequently get invited to have a meal with the person sponsoring that engagement. The thing she always says is, "Well, let's see how we work it around so he has time to exercise." That is a part of the schedule.

A Plan of Action to Reach the Goal

What was my plan of action to reach the goal? The most important thing, of course, was I had to make the commitment. Well, that commitment had been made, and it was a strong one. Limit my sweets. I was not about to completely eliminate sweets. Now, while I was in the process of losing this weight, I had my dessert one day a week after church. I couldn't wait to get over to Braum's place to get that French Chocolate Almond ice cream.

As you know, if you've ever been in an ice cream parlor, there are some scoopers who are better scoopers than others. I mean, some really get the scoops up there, and some are just hesitant about giving you a full scoop. So, I would watch until I could spot the best scooper. If another scooper approached me to dip my ice cream, I'd always have my back turned and then, when I could see that the good scooper was available, I would turn around and I'd say I'd have a double-dip of that Braum's French Chocolate Almond ice cream. It became a goal—get there on Sunday, eat dessert, and then I set the goal to be there again the next Sunday.

I have almost no fried food. I exercise daily, I eat nutritional snacks when I'm up late at night, and I eat a well-balanced diet. I eat slowly, I only eat at the table, and I drink those eight glasses of water every day. Those are the things that have worked for me.

When I had gone through all of the process, then I could put the completion date on it. I can't tell you the number of times I've had somebody say, "Well, you've got to have those goals! As a matter of fact, by next October I'm going have …" and they just set an objective, and then they start trying to work things out in order to reach it on that date. That's a blueprint for disaster, because you become obsessed with that goal and you begin to neglect a whole lot of other things. When you put it together as a program, you might discover that it's unrealistic to have that new automobile by next October. June the following year might be better.

When your goal program is organized, you don't give up the things which are important just to get the things that you really do feel that you want. You look at your goals, you take those specific steps, and then you've got those goals set. When you've done all of that, you have eliminated an awful lot of the unnecessary goals that were there. Now, choose four goals that you can work on every single day.

What do you do with all of the other goals? You might have fifteen or twenty goals left. I've got a number of goals that I cannot work on every day. For example, one of my long-range goals is to play the top 100 golf courses in America before I cash it in and shoot my age before I call it quits on the golf course. Well, I can't go play one of the top golf courses in the world today. Or even next week. But three weeks from today, I'll be playing Oakmont in Pittsburgh, which is one of the top 100 golf courses. Now, have I abandoned that goal because I can't work on it every day? Of course not!

I always write three books at one time. Obviously, I can't be writing three books at one time; what am I talking about? I start the research five years earlier. Every time I see an article or information on this subject, I start filing it away. I clip magazines and newspapers. I might not clip but one a week, or even one a month, but it is in front of me periodically. At least every month I review all of those goals to make certain I've got them there. On a weekly basis, I choose four goals that I'm going to work on every day. With the Performance Planner, I can instantly—in less than two minutes at the end of the week—review it and I can say *it was a good week for this one, a good week for this one; I didn't do very much on this one*, and sometimes that's going to happen. But I am constantly reminded of where I am. This permits me to do more of the things I really want to do.

Now, folks, I can't emphasize this strongly enough. There is no way on earth that you can read this one time and retain everything that has been said. That's the reason you need to keep it with you and read it over and over. That's the reason it needs to become a part of you. I'm going to tell you in advance it is going to require considerable discipline early on. But if you do it for 30 days, I'll absolutely guarantee that you will be elated, delighted, amazed, motivated, enthusiastic, and grateful because you will see changes take place in every phase of your life.

3

REACHING YOUR GOALS
IN LIFE

The question is this: "Ziglar, you say it takes time to set goals. How much time does it take on a daily basis to follow through?" This is a very important question. Here's what it takes me.

The first day of the week, it generally takes me roughly thirty minutes. I do that either Sunday night or early Monday morning. Those thirty minutes are spent figuring out the four most important things I've got to do; the goals I want to work on this week. Each day thereafter, it takes me roughly ten minutes. I keep the Performance Planner with me. If I get up at 5:30, which I frequently do, I keep a schedule by each event: How long I spent doing this and how long I spent doing the other. At the end of the day, I sum it up. Then I can evaluate immediately whether I have accomplished my reasonable objectives for that day. I give myself a grade on each one—either a plus or a minus.

Somebody once asked me, "Do you expect a plus on every one of them every day?" Obviously, I do not. For example, for my social goals, I do not want a plus on every one of them every day. That simply means I would be spending too much time visiting and not getting things done. But, I digress. At the end of the week, I mark the minuses by the ones I do not reach in red. That way, I can look and know instantly whether I've really had an effective week or not.

How to Reach Those Goals

1. Recognize It Will Involve Change

The question is, how do you reach all of those goals? You start by recognizing that this is going to involve change. Now, all change is not progress, but you can put it in the bank that without some change, there's not going to be progress. Can a person change? Yes, of course they can change.

I have a close friend whose name is Ike Reighard. For the first four years of his life, he lived in Appalachia. When he was four years old, his dad, who was a quarry and pulp mill worker, moved them to inner-city Atlanta. Ike became the first member of his family to ever graduate from high school. He decided he was going to go to college. His family thought that was ridiculous. His friends pooh-poohed the idea. Here was a kid from Appalachia, raised primarily in inner-city Atlanta.

"Ike, you're kidding yourself!"

"No, I'm gonna go to college!"

You know what? Ike did go to college. The first year, he flunked out royally. I mean, they invited him not to come back next year. Like a lot of people, Ike said, "Well, no big deal." He did not go back the following year, but instead became a disc jockey at a very low power station. He loaded and unloaded trucks. He did a lot of menial jobs. He was out of school for six years, struggling for survival.

Here's the reason I get so carried away about ongoing education. Ike ended up picking up a copy of *See You at the Top*. For the first time in his life, he learned something about self-image and goals. For the first time in his life, he believed that he could do something with his life. He decided he was going to go back to college. He applied at Mercer University down in Macon, Georgia. They respectfully declined that application. He applied again, and this time, he went there in person to plead his case. They still said no.

"Ike, there's no way! You've been out of high school for six years. You flunked the first go-round miserably; there is no way!"

As he was walking out of the room, terribly despondent, he bumped into Dean Hendricks, the lady who was in charge. She could see he was a troubled young man, so she asked him what the problem was. He literally wept in front of her.

"I want so badly to get my education! I am now ready to get that education. They're not letting me back in."

Well, his openness and, frankly, those tears, played a major part in what happened next.

"OK, Ike. I'm gonna let you in school very conditionally. If you do not maintain a B-average, at the end of this year, your education at Mercer is over."

Two years and three months later, Ike Reighard graduated magna cum laude. Today, within a thirty-minute drive of inner-city Atlanta where Ike Reighard was raised, he pastors one of the fastest-growing churches in this country. Ike Reighard does an awful lot of youth seminars. He is making a dramatic difference in a lot of lives.

Ike's story shows us again and again that you really can change. As you know, I've also made the statement that one definition of insanity is to think you can keep on doing what you've been doing and somehow or another get different results. That simply is not going to work. You've got to have the willingness to change. You've got to have a vision. When Alexander the Great had a vision, he conquered the world. When he lost the vision, he couldn't conquer the liquor bottle. Vision definitely does count. When David had a vision, he conquered Goliath and the Philistines. When he lost the vision, he could not even conquer his own lust.

With that image right, and with your direction set, it's astonishing how many more things you can do.

2. Make a Commitment

You've likely heard me make this statement at least a dozen times: To reach your goals, *you make the commitment*. When you make a commitment, you encounter a problem, and you immediately start looking for a solution to the problem. Without the commitment, you start looking for an escape from that problem. Sam Walton said this: "Commit to your business. I think I overcame every single one of my personal shortcomings by the sheer passion I brought to my work."

3. Build a Solid Foundation

If you're going to reach your goals, all of them, you've got to build a solid foundation. That foundation must be built on integrity and honesty. It's got to be built on the right qualities; otherwise, you might reach *some* of your goals, but you won't reach them all.

A number of years ago, I had the privilege of going atop Calgary Tower in Calgary, Canada. That structure is 626 feet above the ground. Now, I believe in visualizing a lot of things. I cannot visualize without painting a picture, so I asked myself, *How tall is 626 feet?* I knew that was two football fields plus 26 more feet. Then I can say, "Hey, that is *way* up there!" Calgary Tower weighs 13,000 tons—and 7,000 of those tons are underground. When you've got a foundation like that, you can go high.

> **Reach your goals by building a solid foundation on integrity and honesty.**

Alan Bean, one of the astronauts who walked on the moon, is a friend of mine. He's one of the men who stayed on that space platform 57 days as it circled the Earth. He invited us to fly over to watch the blast-off. It was a spectacular sight. I was talking with Alan about that, and he said, "Zig, if you think all of the gear and apparatus was spectacular, you should see what you couldn't see! The tons and tons of concrete from which the blast-off took place is absolutely wonderful. Man, with a foundation like that, you can go anywhere in the world you want to go." The foundation has got to be solid.

A good architect can come to downtown Dallas or downtown LA or anywhere else, and look at the hole in the ground and tell you how big, how wide, how tall the building is going to be. The foundation is the determining factor.

A lot of people today get confused between success and popularity or fame. Madonna has one; Sister Teresa has the other. A lot of people equate success with having a lot of money or getting a lot of recognition, but I know a lot of people with a lot of money who are not very happy. I know a lot of people who get an awful lot of publicity who are not very happy. You might think about the richest man in town, *"Well, that sucker really is a successful individual,"* but when you check up on what he's got, how happy is he? What kind of family relationship does he have? How many friends does he have? How much peace of mind does he have? What I'm talking about here is winning the whole ballgame, and the foundation is the important thing.

4. Ensure Your Attitude

To reach your goals, you've got to ensure your attitude. I've done a lot of talking about attitude. Let me tell you one of the little things I do to make certain my attitude is good: I read the daily paper. I concentrate on the positive things. I turn to the comics section. I also read the sports. You know, in virtually every athletic event, fifty percent of the participants are winners. That's a pretty high winning percentage when you think about it.

How do you build that kind of attitude? It happens when you're growing, when you have your goals set and you're working on them, and when you're building on self-improvement. Now, let me emphasize something. Some people labor under the illusion that you've got to like everything about your job. That you've got to enjoy doing everything about your job. Nothing could be further from the truth! For example, as much as I love my work—and I don't believe there's a human being alive who enjoys doing what they do as much as I enjoy doing what I do—do I like everything about it? No. But, if I've got to do it, now I've got a choice to make. Am I going to do it with the right attitude and get better results, or am I going to gripe and moan and groan and fuss about it and get worse results? *That is the choice I've got to make.*

The decision was already made when you took the job. "Here are some things you gotta do." What you're going to discover is simply this: The better your attitude is while doing the things you don't really like to do, the more likely you are to be given more of the things you do like to do. But everything is not going to be a piece of cake. There are going to be unpleasant things, or things that you don't really like to do.

I think of Tom Hartman and all of those months he spent losing that weight. I know there were an awful lot of times when he did not feel like doing his exercise, carrying all of that weight. Yet, because he'd made the commitment and had the vision, the picture was clear, and he stayed with it. What's the final result? The final result is, of course, not in yet. But I'm telling you, the last time I saw Tom Hartman, he weighed roughly 225 pounds. Now, here's a man, six feet four inches tall, with a large frame. He can easily carry that and not be overweight. He graduated magna cum laude with his degree in psychology. He was counseling battered women, making his contribution to society. He had his own business and was doing infinitely better. He was teaching a Sunday school class every Sunday.

Think about his background for a minute. Initially, he was not happy. The last time I saw him in person, he was not healthy. He was not anything approaching reasonably prosperous, but he is now. However, he had great peace of mind, a tremendous number of friends, and marvelous family relationships. He had tremendous hope that the future was going to be even better. Now I elaborate on that and keep bringing it up for this simple reason: I don't believe there is a person who will ever read this who had as much to overcome in every area of life as Tom Hartman did, and yet by making that commitment and following through, the results have been spectacular. Ensure your attitude.

Did he learn something every time he listened to those audios, for a total of 500 times? Of course not! But he had memorized them. He said he would sit there and he would go right along with me, word for word, verbatim. He was self-talking, and the most important thing you will ever hear is what you say to yourself. He was being encouraged. That's the reason repetition is so important. He made the commitment. He didn't wait to get down; he didn't gamble on it. Every day he did what was necessary to stay up. He was *ensuring his attitude.*

He also made it a habit to do something for somebody else. You know the people I talk with who really are the happiest? Those are the people who are doing things for other people as a matter of course. It is absolutely true, as we have emphasized, that you can have everything you want in life if you will just help enough other people get what they want.

5. Daily Disciplined Accountability

To reach your goals, you've got to have daily disciplined accountability. One hundred and seventy-five former Marines are the CEOs of the Fortune 500 companies. Twenty-six of our presidents served in the military. One of the things they teach in the military, of course, is discipline and commitment. They really do go together.

I've got a close friend; the most positive man I've ever known in my life. His name is Bernie Lofchick. He had quit smoking for five years, and then one day, he said, "Well, you know, it smells so good. One won't hurt!" It took him five years more to get off permanently, and the last time he quit was about fifteen years ago. Don't make exceptions; just be disciplined.

Some psychiatrists say that some alcoholics, under certain conditions, could go back and have a social drink. That borders on insanity! Why gamble something like that? I have seen many cases where a person was sober for a number of years, took that one drink, and they were back off to the races! Watch those exceptions.

I spoke one day in Seattle, Washington. I left Dallas that morning and flew all the way to Seattle. I spoke, then flew back to Dallas. When I got home, by the time I'd collected all my stuff and got ready to hop in bed, it was four o'clock in the morning. My clock was set to get me up at 5:30. It didn't take me long to figure out that's an hour and a half. I don't need to tell you that ninety minutes of sleep is not enough! The clock was already set for 5:30, but as I sat there on the side of the bed, I debated: Do I pull the plug and get up at 5:30, or do I sleep in? *Be smart, Ziglar! Sleep in.* Every fiber of my being said, *don't get up at 5:30.* But I'd made a commitment. I pulled the plug. I got up at 5:30. I did my jogging. I had an absolutely miserable jog and an absolutely horrible day. I was not nearly as productive that day as I usually am. I didn't feel good all day long. I was in bed that night at eight o'clock. Yet, I am going to tell you that one of the most important decisions I have ever made in my life was that I got up that morning at 5:30.

I consider it the most important for this reason: If I had bowed to my human physical, emotional, and mental desire to sleep in, I would have made that exception. A week later, I might have made another exception if I was only going to get four hours of sleep. A week after that, maybe I would have made the exception if I had only gotten seven hours of sleep, and soon the exception becomes the rule. Now, had I slept in, I would have faced that danger.

Watch those exceptions. Do you never make an exception, Zig? Yes, on occasion, you do. But the instant you make that exception, be completely aware of it. Write it down in that Performance Planner and write yourself a little note—WATCH OUT! Because that is a danger signal. That daily disciplined accountability of working can make a difference.

6. Stay in Shape

You need to stay in shape physically, mentally, and spiritually, because man is physical, mental, and spiritual. The interesting thing is that virtually everybody is aware of staying in shape physically. But here is another rather intriguing phenomenon. Despite the fact that we have spent billions and billions of dollars in the last ten years on health programs, exercise programs, diet books, and diet programs, our obesity rate is six percent higher than it was ten years ago. Now, why is that?

If you visualize what you really do want out there, you will look at the benefits from taking care of your health. 92 percent of all the CEOs of major corporations in one major study had a very high energy level. In another study, 90 percent of them exercised regularly; less than 10 percent of them smoked; most of them can tell you their cholesterol level. Integrity is their number one asset; their family is their number one priority. In other words, we keep saying "balance," we keep saying "stay in shape physically, mentally and spiritually."

I'm going to give you four very fast rules.

- ✓ Stay in shape physically.
- ✓ Get enough sleep. Despite what I said a moment ago, this is very important.

- ✓ Start a regular diet and sensible eating and exercise program.
- ✓ Avoid the poisons: drugs, alcohol, and smoking.

When you visualize yourself in those areas, when you see yourself being in better shape, that's when those things do come to be. Failure is the line of least persistence. There's going to come a time in all of our lives when we hit the wall. By that I mean, "I hit the wall! I ran completely out of energy, and that's when I ran on instinct." A lot of times we do that. We do not have any reserve left. And if we've made the commitment—and please don't misunderstand, I think if you're having a heart attack, that's the time to lie down and call the doctor. But so many people quit at the first sign of discomfort. They simply do not hang in there, and hanging in there is very important. When you're in good shape, you can call on that extra energy when you need it. It takes discipline in order to get there.

7. Change Your Vocabulary

If you want to reach your goals, you need to change your vocabulary. I will never forget the spring day I was in Portland, Oregon, jogging on Portland State University campus. The temperature was about 78 degrees. I had a seminar that afternoon, and as I was running that day, all of a sudden I realized something. I was feeling good, and the ground was flowing smoothly beneath my feet. I was breathing easily. Now, the reason I mention that is because for nearly ten months, when that "opportunity clock" would sound off in the morning and I would get up, I can't tell you the number of times I'd gotten up, put my running clothes on, gone outside and while I was running I was just fussing, *Ziglar, what're you tryin' to do? Out here, killin' yourself, acting like a teen-ager! Your buddies are out there, sound asleep in bed, havin' a good time… what're you tryin' to prove?*

Don't you think I didn't tell everybody all over this country about the enormous price I was paying as I would raise my voice and say to them, "Ya' gotta' paaaaayyyy the price!" But I'd made up my mind I was going to do it, and if I said I was going to do it, I was going to do it! I told every friend, relative, neighbor, and complete stranger about this terrible sacrifice I was making. There I was in Portland, Oregon, out there running, and all of a sudden, I was feeling good. I was having a wonderful time, and that was the day I changed my vocabulary.

> **You don't pay the price for success; you enjoy the benefits.**

You don't pay the price for good health; you enjoy the benefits of good health. You don't pay the price for success; you pay the price for failure and enjoy the benefits of success. You don't pay the price for a good marriage; you enjoy the benefits of a good marriage. You pay the price for a bad one.

When we look at it in that light and discipline ourselves to keep on doing it, the day's going to come when, instead of it being a chore, it gets to be fun. I believe you can make almost any job fun to do.

Up in North Carolina, there is a chicken plucking plant that uses the attitude session of what we're talking about. As a young-ster, I was a butcher. When you pull the feathers off one chicken, and when you clean all those chickens out, the inside of one chicken looks just like the inside of all other chickens! Here's a group of people who clean those chickens all day every day, at minimum wage in virtually every case. They started talking and developing those people who were cleaning those chickens! They started giving them ear sets and motivational recordings and the workers started listening. What would happen was they'd be listening along, and then I'd put a funny on them, and they would just laugh and then, man, they'd go back to cleaning those chickens. Productivity went up substantially. Turnover reduced substantially. Profits increased substantially.

What am I saying? Everybody is subject to getting excited when they're having some fun, when we're taking an interest in them, and when we're developing that interest. We've gotten business from people because the owner of that plant went all over that part of North Carolina and he was speaking at Lions and Rotaries and telling them what his hourly workers were doing. See, so many times we think, "Well, now, that person's not interested in that kinda stuff," or "You can't motivate that person!" Hey! Let me tell you something. When people have fun doing what they're doing, they're going to do a better job. Again, that's not to say that everything can be fun. You just need to change your vocabulary.

8. Break Down the Goal.

You need to break the goal in pieces if you're going to reach the goal. After I left the Cooper Clinic, they said to me, "Here's what you need to do." I looked at it, and I'd planned on losing the weight in ten months, I figured that's how long it was going to take me to write the book. I needed to lose 37 pounds, so I divided that, and I said, "Well, all I gotta do is lose three and seven-tenths pounds a month." Now, that's no big deal. That's less than a pound a week! I knew I could do it! I was so confident of it I didn't even bother to get started for 28 days!

See, that's one of the major problems in life.

"Here are your quotas for six months."

"Hey! That's no big deal! It's just February 23rd, man! I got plenty of time!"

The next thing you know it's March 22nd, then it's April 15th.

"Oh, it's too late now! But next year… I'll guarantee ya'!" You've got to get in high gear!

I looked at it again and discovered that in order to lose the 37 pounds, all I had to do was lose one and nine-tenths ounces a day, on average, every day for ten months. That book *See You at the Top* has 384 pages in it. I wrote it in ten months. That means on average I wrote one and one-fourth pages a day every day for ten months.

Let me tell you how to raise positive kids in a cynical world. Let me tell you how to build a magnificent relationship with your mate. Let me tell you how to move to the top of the corporate ladder. Let me tell you how to become a world-class professional salesperson, a counselor, or educator, or whatever it is that you want to be. It is not the monumental tasks you do for one week or one month. It is those daily things you do every day. The commitment every day. *Today I'm going to take this step or that step. I'm going to make this kind of progress every day.* It's the little things that make a difference. A minute can make a difference.

9. Be a Team Player

You have to join the team; you have to work with others. When I was a youngster down in Yazoo City, Mississippi, there were some abandoned railroad tracks, and us kids used to go over there and see which one could walk the furthest on those tracks. We'd walk a few steps and fall off. If we would have just joined hands across the rails, we literally could have walked as far as the tracks went by supporting and balancing each other. You have to have the team concept because, you see, we've talked a lot about the fact that job security no longer exists. But employment security is a thing of an entirely different nature. The better team player you are, the better individual you are, the better performer you are, the more likely you are to have that employment security.

Have you ever seen a flock of Canadian geese flying overhead? If you follow them very far, you will notice three things about flocks of geese: They always fly in a V-formation. You will also notice that one leg of the V is a little longer than the other leg. Lastly, as you follow them across the horizon, there appears to be periodically some confusion in the flock. Have you ever wondered why one leg of that V is always longer than the other leg? It's longer because it has more geese in it.

Incidentally, a few years ago, some psychologists studied geese, and they discovered that when you hear them honkin', they're not just honkin' Dixie. Those are motivational honks. Those are encouragement honks. They're saying, "Come on, Bill, you know, Charlie Brown's farm is just four miles down the road! Man, you can make it! Hang in there. It's downwind all the way!"

One of the reasons they say that is because of the loyalty the geese have for each other. If one of them gets hurt or sick; a companion will stay with them until they either recover or die. Loyalty is a moral principle there.

Why do geese fly in V-formation? Well, wind tunnel tests revealed that when they fly in the V-formation they set up a partial vacuum off of either wing, and the flock can literally fly

73 percent further than the individual goose can fly. Teamwork. The reason there appears to be that confusion from time to time is because the lead goose, in fighting that headwind, grows weary more quickly and they change the leader's position frequently. They cooperate and work together.

10. Learn How to Train Fleas

If you are going to reach your goals, you have to learn how to train fleas by putting them in a jar. If you put the top on, fleas will jump up, and they'll hit the top—over and over and over. You watch them jump, and then suddenly you will notice that though they continue to jump, they are no longer hitting the top. Then you can take the top off, and they will continue to jump, but they cannot jump out of the jar. The reason they cannot jump out of the jar is because they have conditioned themselves to jump just so high.

Man is exactly the same way. Man starts out in life with dreams to write the book, to break the record, to climb the mountain, to do something significant. Along the way, he bumps his head, stubs his toe, or makes some mistakes. Then, all of a sudden, he loses that marvelous concentration, confidence,

Don't become a SNIOP

and creativity and becomes a S-N-I-O-P. That's a person who is Susceptible to the Negative Influence of Other People.

The classic example is the four-minute mile. For years and years, athletes said, "I'm gonna break the four-minute barrier." But when they made that statement, the coaches would get their stopwatches out and say, "Man, you might get it down to 4.02, but you'll never break that barrier!" For years and years, athletes tried valiantly to do it but could not.

Then, one day, a flea trainer named Roger Bannister from Britain ran a mile in less than four minutes. Almost immediately after him, Landy of Australia broke the four-minute barrier, and since then over 500 individuals have run that race in less than four minutes, including a high school student and a 37-year-old man.

This year, John Walker of New Zealand, who has run over 130 sub-four-minute miles, is now 40 years old. He's in training right now to break the barrier again. There have been at least six different races where eight young men, all in that same race, broke the four-minute barrier. Is it because they all of a sudden got that much better physically? Did the equipment improve that much? It might have improved some, but when Roger Bannister, who followed every principle of goal-setting that I'm talking about here, took his shot at it, he measured every stride. He is a superb athlete. He got in marvelous condition, and he recruited three other guys to serve him as pacers in that race, and he had targets along the way. He knew how long his strides were, how many he could jog or run in 440. He broke it all down. When he broke the barrier, athletes all over the world realized it was not a physiological barrier; it was a psychological barrier. That's an important difference.

Flea trainers, in case you're missing the point, are people who literally jump out of the jar. Flea trainers don't tell other people where to get off; they show them how to get on. Flea trainers understand that you don't try to see through people—you try to see people through. Flea trainers understand that *you can have everything in life you want if you will just help enough other people get what they want.*

Do you want to reach your goals? You've got to have that flea trainer attitude. You've got to understand those principles, that just because somebody else did or didn't, it has nothing whatsoever to do with your ability. I have seen it happen so many times, where, for example, a salesperson breaks a record. Then somebody comes along and says, "If she can, I can." Whatever we're doing, the example that somebody else sets serves as an inspiration. That's the reason I tell so many stories. In addition, the Center for Creative Research in Greensboro, North Carolina, has discovered beyond any doubt that the parable, the story, is the best way to teach. Of course, that's something somebody else told us about two thousand years ago, isn't it?

11. See the Reaching

To reach your goals, you literally have to *see the reaching*. Jack Nicklaus says he gets his best golf practice in on his way to the golf course. He has a detailed outline of the course itself, and he sees every shot before he ever hits. He sees the ball going in the hole.

I saw myself doing exactly what I'm doing way back yonder in 1952. It took me sixteen more years before I could do it on a full-time basis, and in those sixteen years, I had to do a lot of other things. I was a salesperson to support my family. But the dream—the vision—never left me. I could see myself there. When I hung the picture of that fella in the Jockey shorts in my bathroom on the mirror, I literally saw him hundreds and hundreds of times, and I kept saying, "Now, that's the way I am going to be." I could literally see the reaching. This is so enormously important.

A number of years ago, when ships were sailing the seas, a young sailor was ordered aloft to trim the sails because a squall was coming up. When he was climbing up, he made the mistake of looking down. The turbulence of the sea and the roll of the ship caused him to become nauseated, and he started to lose his balance. An older sailor underneath him said, "Look up, son! Look up!" He looked up and regained his balance. The message is clear: If the outlook is not looking good, try the uplook. It's always good.

Helen Keller put it so eloquently when she said, "If you keep your eyes on the sun, you will not see the shadows." We need to see ourselves as already being there. We need to see ourselves in our relationship with our mate as a happy one. We need to see ourselves with our children in a good relationship. We need to see our students in the proper light, and we will deal with them altogether differently. You treat people exactly like you see them, and the way you treat them has a direct bearing on their performance.

I can tell you that as a parent, a parent's expectations have a direct bearing on our child's performance. I can tell you as an employer, that an employer's expectations have a direct bearing on their performance. I can tell you as an educator that my expectations of those I'm teaching have a direct bearing on their performance. If you're going to reach those goals, you need to do it now.

Tomorrow has been described as the greatest labor-saving device of all time. We use it a lot of times. "I'm gonna do this tomorrow." "I'm gonna do this when I have time." "I'm gonna do this when…" The truth of the matter is, the present is now. The future is also now. We need to get into action. The reason I did such a strong job of selling you on having goals is because I know that if you take action now, you're going to be infinitely more successful and far more likely to reach your goals. If you have those goals, if you can see them, then that's when things are going to happen. But you have to get started now.

Success is a Journey

One of my favorite examples is the story of Andy Gardner. He's a young man who works with Merrill-Lynch. They say that they've got more people every year who earn $100,000, as much as, maybe more, than any other company in America. Andy is now an assistant vice president with them, and he said, "Zig, they literally come in all sizes, they come in all shapes, and they come in all colors. They're extroverts and introverts. They're male and female. They have tremendously varied educational backgrounds. Some of them offer the complete menu; others are specialists. There is one thing that they all have in common: You call them at 2:30 in the afternoon on February 22nd and ask them, 'Where are you on your goals?' they can tell you exactly where they are, to the penny. You call them on March 23rd or November 26th or any other day. That is one thing every one of them has. They're very definite. They're very specific in their goals. If they're earning a six-figure income, you can absolutely count on it."

Andy Gardner said to me, "Zig, I started listening to you a number of years ago. Here's what I discovered. You and I come from a different generation. We have different political views. We have different social views. We have different religious views. But the principles you're talking about are so universal that I adopted every one of them and am following them as a part of my life."

When Andy joined Merrill-Lynch, one of the first objectives they have is to make the Executive Club. That's kind of like a rookie club, and if you can make it early on, that represents a considerable amount of recognition and accomplishment. His manager was a man named Parks Duncan. Andy said that Parks called him in one day and Andy thought, "You know, at that point, I wasn't on schedule to make anybody's club! Parks got to talking to me, 'Andy, let me tell you what I'm going to do.' He said, 'I believe you have every ability to make the Executive Club. I want to show you where your new office is going to be. We're building it; it's about a half-mile from here. Here's the blueprint, and here is your office.'"

Andy said he left there and was so excited that he skipped lunch and walked the half-mile over to the new office building. There was nothing but a frame and a lot of concrete and some girders. He knew exactly where it was. He said, "Only the floor was in. I got there, and I literally squatted down as if I were at my desk in my new office. I looked out, and the view there was marvelous! I visualized my sales assistant outside, answering the phone, saying, 'Yes, this is Mr. Gardner's office.' I could see all of that in my own mind." Now, this is the visualization I'm talking about. Andy said, "When I left there I had that dream; I had a vision. Yes, I was going to make the Executive Club! In the month of November, I more than doubled my daily production. I was just so excited! I was on schedule to make it."

Then he said, "Early in December, three of my big deals washed out. It was at that point that some of my associates started saying to me, 'Well, Andy, what you really ought to do is start concentrating on next year. Have a good year for the rest of this year.' But, by then, it was undeniably impossible for me to give up. I took that renewed effort, and I started going over to my new office I was going to be in every day, and the vision became more real all the time. It's amazing how things started popping into place. The goal was to get there by December 21st. On December 21st, that's exactly when I hit my goal." *Visualization absolutely does work.*

This happened to Andy back in 1984. Three years later, he moved to Houston, and for two and a half years he managed an office there. He made the President's Club in 1991, and then he said, "You know, Zig, I felt like I needed an explosion." He came to Dallas and spent three days with us in June of 1992. In June 1992, despite the fact that he had lost three days from productivity, he gained an altogether larger picture of himself, and his vision emerged. As a result of that, not only did he make the infinitely prestigious President's Club, in that month of June he broke his best record ever by over 80 percent. In July, he almost broke the June record, and August was a repeat of the same thing. Since then, he set another goal, and when that happened, he said, "In 1992, I'm going to win the *Win Smith Fellow Award*." Now, that's the ultimate with Merrill-Lynch. He accomplished that objective, and he reached that particular goal.

Let me emphasize something that is very important. If he would have set the goal of being a Win Smith Fellow winner first, that would have been absolutely insane. He had no experience, and a very small base to work from. He was just getting started. There were many things he did not know. So, he set a more reasonable goal. It was still a big goal, but it wasn't out of sight. He made the Executive Club.

What is my point? The three best years this guy ever had were in 1990, 1991, and 1992. As you know, those have not been the best economic years in our society. That goes right back to something I've been saying all the way through. Success is not out there, ladies and gentlemen. Success is right here between your ears.

Again, let me say it: I don't care how good times are, there are some people who literally are going to foul them up—financially. I don't care how bad times are; there are some people who are going to do well regardless. I've noticed that trend since the Depression way back yonder in the 1930s. I believe that if you'll take the steps we've been discussing and follow the procedure in setting the goals, success can be yours.

As you start on this journey, there are going to be some people that you will encounter as did Andy Gardner, Pam Lontos, and Ike Reighard. There are going to be some people who will laugh at you and say, "Man, you can't do it!" Let me remind you: The little world laughed, but the big world was on the banks of the Hudson when Fulton went steaming by.

As you reach the destination that some did not believe you could make, let me give the strongest reference to it I can, the importance of it.

What you become is more important than what you get.

What you get by reaching your goals is not nearly as important as what you will *become* by reaching your goals. And that is the winner you were born to be.

4

MOTIVATION+INFORMATION= INSPIRATION

Let me tell you what one of my objectives is today. It's kind of like this ol' boy back home. He was caught in a flash flood. It was an instant one, and he was up on the rooftop of his house. One of his neighbors came floating by, and he said, "John, this flood's just terrible, isn't it?"

John said, "No, it ain't that bad!"

"Whaddya mean, it's not that bad? Why, there goes your hen-house floatin' downstream right now!"

"I know that. But we started raisin' ducks just a few months ago and see, there they are, every one of 'em just swimmin' around. Everything gonna be alright."

"Yeah, but this high water's gonna ruin your crops."

"My crops were already ruined anyhow. Not gonna have any impact. We need a little irrigation. This takes care of that."

Well, you know, some people persist in being negative. He said, "Yeah, but look! The water's risin'! First thing you know it's gonna be up to your windows."

"Man, I hope it gets there! They're so dirty they need washin'!"

What I am really saying is that we can look at things through two different pairs of eyes—the optimist's eyes, or the cynical eyes. Today, we're going to be looking at winning through persistence, enthusiasm, and desire.

An old minister was once asked the question as to why he was so effective. He said, "Well, basically, I tell people what I'm going to tell them. Then I tell them, and then I tell them what I told them." You'll hear me say over and over that repetition is the mother of learning. That makes it the father of action and the architect of accomplishment.

The Center for Creative Research in Greensboro, North Carolina, has discovered what some have known for literally a couple of thousand years: The best way to teach is through a parable. We remember when we identify, and we're going to extract lessons from each one of the stories we read.

A few years ago, I had an opportunity to speak over at Hinds Community College in Raymond, Mississippi. I had gone to school there back in 1943, and a man there named Jobie Harris had a profound impact on my life. I was helping them raise money to establish a Jobie and Jim El Harris scholarship fund.

The morning I spoke at the college, the auditorium was absolutely packed. The students, faculty, and visitors from in town were standing all the way around the back. As I started speaking, I could not help but notice that on the very front row there were seven empty seats, and on the second row, there were five empty seats. I said to the people who were standing, "We have seven empty seats right down here and five over here. Why don't you come on down and take a comfortable seat for this presentation? All you gotta do is walk fifteen or twenty steps, and you're here."

Only one person came on down to occupy that front row. I said to the group, "I wish it were possible for me to reach down, if I were strong enough and had the time, to literally take these seats up and move them to the back to give them to you, but I'm just not that strong. We don't have that kind of time, and I'm certain the administration would not smile at me doin' that if I could! The seats are available, but you've gotta take the steps to get there.

"Now, on the second row, there are some obstacles you gotta overcome because these five seats happen to be in the middle of the row. But these look like congenial people; they might even help you get past that particular obstacle. That's life itself. Because whatever you get in life, there are going to be some obstacles that stand between you and them, but it's up to you to take the steps."

It was quite an experience for me. The message I'm delivering to you now is that front-row seats are available, but you have to go claim them. If there are some obstacles along the way, you've got to climb those obstacles.

We have a tremendous need in America today for front-row people. But remember something which I believe is very basic: It's awfully tough to be successful when things are too easy. In a previous book, I made reference to the fact that of the 300 world-class leaders, such as Churchill, Roosevelt, Helen Keller, Martin Luther King, Mahatma Gandhi, etc., 75 percent of them had either been abused as children, had some severe physical disability, or were raised in poverty. It is tough to be successful when things are too easy.

I had an interesting experience over in Columbia, South Carolina. I met a young man in the motel there named Fernando Quintero. Now, Fernando is from Mexico. He lived in San Diego for a year and a half. While living there, he worked with, went to school with and associated only with people who spoke Spanish. The bottom line is that at the end of the year and a half, he could not speak any English. There was no need to, in his mind. He then moved to Columbia, South Carolina, where three months later he was speaking English, and six months later he was very fluent in the language. Because in Columbia, nobody there spoke any Spanish and he had to learn English.

My daughter-in-law, who is an extraordinarily bright young woman, spent a year in New Orleans. She's from Campeche, Mexico. All of her friends spoke Spanish; the school was conducted in Spanish for the English Spanish. She could not speak any English. Then she came to Austin College, where she met my son. She finished the end of the first year with a 3.0. You see, she had to learn English!

Now, what am I saying? I'm saying that a lot of times we don't have people who require us to do things, but if we want to get the most out of life, then we have got to require those things all by ourselves. Life is easier when you are tough on yourself. But when you're easy on yourself, life is enormously tough.

Happiness is a Choice

Our rewards for doing the things we've been talking about are enormous. Now, what does everybody want? Well, everybody wants to be happy, they want to be healthy, they want to be at least reasonably prosperous, they want to be secure, they want to have friends, they want to have peace of mind, they want to have good family relationships, and they want to have hope.

The question then comes up, can you really set happiness as being a goal? It's an intriguing question. Let's answer it.

Rose Barthel says this: "Happiness is a conscious choice; it is not an automatic response." Happiness is an attitude. Let me also say that happiness is not a *when* and a *where*; it is a *here* and a *now*.

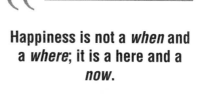

Happiness is not a *when* and a *where*; it is a here and a now.

Many people say they're going to be happy *when* they get in the house, but they won't. They think they'll be happy when they get everything properly arranged. But they won't. They'll be happy when the landscaping is completed, but they won't. Then they will be happy when they build a patio out back, but they really won't. Then they'll be happy when they get the mortgage paid off, but they really won't. Then they'll be happy when they have the second home.

A lot of people are going to be happy on a *when* or a *where*. "Ohhhh! When we get out to Hawaii for that ten-day vacation, man, then I'm gonna be happy!" That is not the way it is, because it makes no difference where you go—there you are. Let me say it again: It doesn't make any difference where you go because there you are. Until you are happy with you, you're not going to be happy with what you have or where you are.

I love what Dennis Prager in a *Reader's Digest* article had to say about this. He said, "Fun is what we experience during an act. Happiness is what we experience after an act. It is a deeper, more abiding emotion." He says things like "going to an amusement park or ball game, watching a movie or television, are fun activities. They help us relax. They help us temporarily forget our problems and maybe even laugh. But they do not bring happiness because their positive effect ends when the fun ends. Happiness is of much longer duration." Mr. Prager also points out with unusual insight that, "The people who cling to the belief that a fun-filled, pain-free life equals happiness actually diminish their chances of ever attaining real happiness. If fun and pleasure equated with happiness, then pain must be equated with unhappiness, but, in fact, the opposite is true. More times than not, things that lead to happiness involve some pain."

Now, let me say that he's absolutely right. Happiness is not pleasure—it's victory. It's a victory over things that are tough; a victory over odds that seem to be insurmountable. That doesn't mean I don't think we ought to have some fun. I love the story about Dallas Theological Seminary. They had a serving line over there, and at the beginning of the line, they had apples, and there was a little sign that said, "Take only one apple. God is watching." They got to the end of the line where they had the chocolate chip cookies, and another little sign said, "Take as many as you want. God is busy watching the apples." I believe we need to have a little fun as we go along.

But let's explore this thing about happy a little further and see what we can do about it. I'll ask you to answer these questions in your own mind:

Do you believe that your happiness has anything to do with your health? In other words, if you're healthy and feeling good, will that increase your chances of happiness?

Do you believe that if you were at least prosperous enough that you didn't have to worry, you had a flat tire or the plumbing fouled up or something like that, could that be a contributing factor in being happy?

Do you believe that if you're confident in what you do, secure in the knowledge that as long as you perform you're going to have your job, that that too would be a factor in your happiness?

Do you believe that if you have a lot of loyal friends that will help make you happy?

How about peace of mind? If you have that resolved, do you believe that would make you happy?

How about good family relationships? Does your family have anything to do with your happiness?

Here's the big question: Do you honestly believe there's something you can do about your health, your prosperity, your security, your friends, your peace of mind, and your good family relationships? Won't that give you hope for the future? Isn't it true that hope has something to do with your happiness? Do you believe that *yes, there is something I can do about setting happiness as my goal because it can be a by-product of all the other things*? Does that make any sense? I don't know how you feel about that, but when I got really involved in this thinking process, I got enormously excited because I believe for an awful lot of people this is going to represent a breakthrough!

Why do I say that? Because things we have no control over can also make us unhappy, but when we come right back down the list, we can say, "I can do something about that, I can do something about this." Now we go right back to work on regaining part of what we lost. Man, I get excited about that!

Let's go down the list and look at the statement we make so many times, that *you can have everything in life you want if you will just help enough other people get what they want.* I'm talking philosophy; I'm not talking tactic. Let me give you a personal example. Many years ago, when I entered the world of selling at the ripe old age of 21, the first two and a half years we just about starved to death—I mean, things were really tough. Then, thanks to a man named P.C. Merrell, we had a dramatic turnaround. My business exploded.

I finished that year out as the number two salesman out of over 7,000. The company had, every year at the end of August, a National Booster Week. They encouraged every salesperson to pull out all the stops; work eighteen hours a day, make every possible call, give extra bonuses to the hostesses, "Let's really do it up! The biggest week in the year, let's make it National Booster Week!"

Well, the first two years, I didn't get excited about Booster Week because I was struggling to eat. But I was primed, and I hit the ground running on this particular week. I was in the cookware business. I cooked pancakes every morning that week. I prepared a salad every day at lunch for a prospect, then I put on a dinner demonstration in the evening. That week I sold two and a half times as much as I had ever sold in any week prior. Man, I tell you, I was motivated! As a matter of fact, I took the Redhead and our only daughter down to Jackson, Mississippi to be with her family because the convention following Booster Week was to be in Biloxi and I wanted to be able to do nothing but work.

In all fairness, the company only encouraged us to maintain that kind of schedule one week out of the year. They explained, like a rubber band which is useful only when it's stretched, when you really stretch out sometimes, that's when you can determine your capability of doing great things. I finished making my last call on Saturday night, and it was about ten o'clock. I drove to

Atlanta, Georgia, and saw Bill Cranford, the man who brought me into the business.

"Zig, stop by here, catch a few hours' sleep before you drive on."

I woke ol' Bill up about 2:30 or 3:00 in the morning. He got out of bed, made the coffee, and we sat there until 5:30. For those two and one-half hours, let me tell you what I was doing. I had made 39 sales calls that week. I had made 34 sales, and I took Bill Cranford from *hello* to *goodbye* in every single one of those experiences!

"Bill, they said this an' I said that an' they did this an' I did that and, man! They bought!"

Thirty-nine calls, and I went all the way through. Nonstop. As you know, I speak at about 280 words a minute with gusts up to about 550, so I covered an awful lot of territory! Finally, about 5:30, all of a sudden it hit me.

"Oh, my goodness, Bill! How are *YOU* doing?"

I had not asked him one single question; had not inquired about his health, his family, his life, his business, his nothing! I had totally dominated the conversation. I had the worst case of "*I trouble*" I think anybody has ever had in their life!

I said, "Bill, I am embarrassed. I apologize."

Bill Cranford said something to me that impacted my life and affected my thinking dramatically.

He said, "Zig, don't give it a thought. I have thoroughly enjoyed every moment of what you had to say. Now, let me remind you of something. I'm the one who brought you into this business. I'm the one who trained you. I'm the one who encouraged you when you were discouraged. I'm the one who took you out in the field and specifically worked with you, holding your hand. You see, Zig, until you've experienced what I just experienced, you'll never know what real happiness and real success are. The delight I have received by your success is infinitely greater than the delight you're experiencing by having that success."

The man was entirely, 100 percent right! Was he a happy man? You absolutely can count on it.

Changing Your Mind = Prosperity and Success

Let's look at *prosperity*. I was raised working in a grocery store down in Yazoo City, Mississippi. It was during the Depression, and we had a very limited inventory. Ninety percent of all of the business that was done in that grocery store was done from four o'clock on Friday afternoon until eleven o'clock on Saturday night—that's when everybody got paid. Merchants carried minimal inventory, and we frequently ran out of what we were selling, so we borrowed from the other merchants.

There was a young man named Charlie Scott, who worked across the street. He was their runner for that store as I was the runner for the store I worked in. Many times, Charlie would hit our front door in a dead run, and he would say to our owner, "Mr. Anderson, I need to borrow a half-dozen cans of tomatoes."

"Well, Charlie, you know where they are. Go get 'em!"

Charlie, in a dead run, would go back to the shelf where the tomatoes were. He'd scoop up six cans, he would run back up to the counter, plop them down and sign his name, indicating he'd gotten the six cans of tomatoes, and he would scoot out the front door.

One day I asked Mr. Anderson, "Why on Earth does Charlie Scott always run everywhere?"

"Well, Charlie's working for a raise, and he's going to get it, too!"

"Mr. Anderson, how do you know Charlie Scott's going to get a raise?"

"I know Charlie Scott's going to get a raise because if the man he's working for doesn't give it to him, I will!"

You see, ladies and gentlemen, you've probably heard me talk about employment security before. The reality is, you work for yourself, regardless of who signs the check. And when you give that big of an effort, then things are going to happen.

A few years ago, I spoke at Mississippi State University. I told that story, and when it was over, a guy—a tall, slender fella—came up to me and said, "Let me ask you—when was the last time you saw Charlie Scott?"

I said, "Well, Charlie's two years older than I am, so that means he left Yazoo City in 1942 to go into the service. I haven't seen him since then."

"You probably wouldn't even recognize him, would ya'?"

"No, I wouldn't."

"I didn't think so. I'm Charlie Scott."

Charlie Scott retired at age 50. He was successful in every area of his life because he took those habits he had acquired in childhood—which was a tough one—and applied them all his life. Because of that, he was able to accomplish the objectives we are talking about.

When we talk about the secure individual, where does the security come from? Security determines the way you handle situations in life, particularly in your relationships. I love this story about an experience Buddha had. A man met him on the street one day and began to call him mean and ugly names. Buddha listened quietly and thoughtfully until the man ran out of epithets and had to pause for breath.

"If you offer something to a man and he refuses it, to whom does it belong?" asked Buddha.

The spiteful man replied, "It belongs, I suppose, to the one who offered it."

Then Buddha said, "The abuse and vile names you offer me I refuse to accept." The detractor turned and walked away.

A secure individual is never made to feel inferior by the insecure people of life; those fault-finders and backbiters and ne'er-do-wells and critics. How do you determine what makes a person secure? Well, over and over I've said you are what you are and where you are because of what's gone into your mind. You change what you are; you change where you are, by changing what goes into your mind.

> **Change what you are and where you are by changing what goes into your mind.**

How do you get friends? Well, the best way to get friends is to be a friend. Those people who go out looking for friends, they're scarce. But when you go out in life to be a friend, you'll find them everywhere. The Bill Cranford attitude will enable people to have more friends.

What is peace of mind? One of the men whom I have great respect for, a young man named Peter Lowe, who does seminars that I speak on all over the country, was going to buy his mother-in-law a little business. As he analyzed these businesses, in 22 straight instances, he would ask them, "Do you have another set of books?" Twenty-two of them responded, "Yes, I do." Peter would look at that other set of books, and he said, "You know, Zig, the sad thing is the amount they were stealing from the government was very little, maybe a thousand dollars, or five thousand dollars. But can't you just imagine the grief and the turmoil they go through every time an official-looking government agent comes walking in and makes that announcement... 'I'm from the government, and I'm here to help!'"

I know a lot of you know exactly what I'm talking about! So, these individuals do not have peace of mind. How much more productive would they have been had they played it straight and were able to utilize all their creative resources? I believe it makes a dramatic difference. Peace of mind for me comes when I understand where I will spend eternity.

I was excited to read last week that ninety percent of people in America believe in God. That's exciting! Now, if we can persuade them to *believe* God, then we really will have something to be excited about!

Hope Leads to Change

Good family relationships are so enormously important, and everything we've been talking about has to do with that, but I'm going to get back to that a little bit later. And, of course, hope. If you've got all these things, then the hope can be legitimate.

What is hope? It's the fuel which propels the engine of effort through the difficult times and over the obstacles which regularly appear on the roadway to success.

All these things constitute a package. That's what this really amounts to. If you want these things, then you must plan for them.

Total success demands responsibility. It demands that you accept responsibility for your conduct and your performance because each of them has consequences. I love this little bit by Robert Orben: Two parents were comparing notes. One said, "I'm really concerned. Our kids are getting into so much trouble! I don't think the daycare center, nursery school, after-school program, and babysitters are raising them right!" That really does say something, doesn't it? Responsibility is what I'm talking about here.

Understand something: Winners don't always finish first. You see, there is confusion in our society that unless you are the absolute best and you win every time, you're not a winner. Winners do not always finish first, but they do give their best effort. I happen to believe that in the 1994 Super Bowl XXVII, one of the real winners was a member of the Buffalo Bills' football team. It was a blowout. Everybody knows that I'm a dyed-in-the-wool Dallas Cowboys fan. We were leading 52-17 when suddenly, there was a fumble. It hit the ground, bounced up, and Leon Lett grabbed the ball and lumbered toward the end zone. He got within twenty yards, and I watched the replay to make absolutely certain that I had my yardage right. When Leon Lett was on the ten-yard-line, he started hot-doggin' it big time, you know, prancing over, holding his football out there. When Leon was on the ten-yard-line, Don Beebe, the outstanding wide receiver for the Buffalo Bills, was on the twenty-yard-line. He made up ten yards on Leon in less than twenty yards. He slapped the ball away, and we did not get the other touchdown.

Don Beebe knew that there was no way that the Bills had a chance to win that game. But effort, personal pride ... *everything* was at stake as far as he was concerned. Coincidentally, by him doing that, it helped his team to avoid having the biggest loss ever in Super Bowl history. He had hope and gave his best.

What am I saying? You win, ladies and gentlemen, when you give it that best effort.

A lot of times in life, things happen over which we have no control. In 1986, Penn State and Notre Dame were playing, and Penn State was ahead. Notre Dame had the ball, and they were driving down to the end of the field. Their tight end got loose in the end zone, and the quarterback hit him letter-perfect right in the hands. He dropped the ball. Had he caught the ball, Notre Dame would have won—but he dropped the ball. Penn State won and went on to win the national championship.

Now here's the message. You see, ten players on the Notre Dame team had done everything they were supposed to. They filled their assignments to perfection. But one person dropped the ball.

I don't care what your job is; I don't care how circumstances are with you in your home, in your school, in your job, in the factory or wherever. There are going to be a number of occasions where you're going to do everything you're supposed to, and somebody else is going to drop the ball. We've got to learn to deal with the dropped balls of life. This attitude, this image we're making of ourselves really does make the difference.

The question is, do we respond to life, or do we react to life? Response, as you know, is positive; reaction is negative. Success in the '90s demanded change, and it demanded creativity. There are an awful lot of people who resist that change.

Motivation plus information equals inspiration. Because

> **Motivation plus information equals inspiration.**

creativity is so important, I want to share with you something that came to me this very week. I've been incredibly excited about it because it really says something.

In our first recording seminar in this series, Mary Ellen Caldwell was here, and during one of the breaks, she came up to me and said, "Look at what I've got!" She showed me a list of a number of things she was going to be doing to encourage her dad, who had been forced into retirement against his will at age 65. She said, "Dad really has lost heart. He's not excited about life. He's frustrated. He doesn't feel there's any use for him, and look! You have given me all of these ideas!" Well, the reality is, I had not talked about retirement. I had not given her any ideas at all! What on Earth had happened?

Let me diagram for you of what I believe happened, because I believe this is the key to so many of the mysteries of life and why people do not do more with themselves. Number one, what Mary Ellen had done was to take her lifetime of information and experience and learned from it all.

Here is a little bit of intriguing and subjective information. I don't know how you could possibly prove it, but I believe it has validity. Two of the most brilliant PhDs I've ever known in my life told me this five years apart; if you have your Ph.D., then less than one-half of one percent of your total knowledge inventory came in a formal education environment. Don't misunderstand me; I'm not saying that's not important! The first thing you do is you learn to read, and then you read to learn. As I'll talk about later, you will learn to read people as well.

In her lifetime, Mary Ellen had a tremendous number of experiences and so forth, that's number one. Second, she had a deep love and a concern for her dad. Third, she was involved in personal growth seminars. Let's see if we can bring some light together about what happened. Motivation, you see, is the spark that lights the fire of knowledge. The more you already know, and the broader your base is, the more new ideas and information will benefit you. In order to make it work, you need to take some quiet time and put it all together. Let me tell you what happened.

I was having dinner with my friend and mentor, Fred Smith. During the course of the evening, as always, I had my notepad with me. I make sure to carry a notepad when I am going to spend time with Fred. He always puts something heavy on me. That night, he said one thing that got me real excited. He said, "Zig, remember that great learners are not always great thinkers." I got to reflecting on that. I was over in Tampa, Florida, and I'd been in the dental chair for about five hours that day. I had decided I wasn't going to do my exercise, but I wanted to go for a stroll. I had a very casual forty-minute walk, followed by a very quiet dinner. Then I got to reflecting on this thing called "motivation." You see, to motivate is to pull out or draw out that which is on the inside, and motivation plus information equals inspiration. All of a sudden, things came together, and I got so excited because it explained what had happened to Mary Ellen Caldwell, and that means it explains what happens to us every day of our lives.

Mary Ellen took the information she had accumulated over a long period of time and stored it. Then, I gave her some brand-new information, which got her excited. What happened? Up popped information she thought she had forgotten about because she hadn't used it. At the same time, up popped the information that I'd just given her; they took a look at each other, and they said, "Hey! I like you! Do you like me?" They both said, "Yeah! Let's get together!" A marriage service was performed, and a complete birth of brand-new ideas took place. That, to me, is tremendously exciting!

What am I saying? I'm saying that in addition to all the information you get, there are those times when we must be absolutely quiet. We've got to be thinking about what we're dealing with. When we think about what we're dealing with, it's amazing what's going to happen. Now, you regularly need the motivational input to bring new information in, which stirs up the old information. Both of them come to the front, get together, and create new ideas. That's one of the reasons that I say the following in my books and my audios: As valuable as motivational audios are, there are those occasions when you do not want to have them or anything else playing. For example, when you're walking, instead of listening to music or motivation or something of that nature, think about your business or something you're wrestling with. It's truly amazing how many times brand new ideas will be born to you if you just get silent.

Mary Ellen had put together things she thought she had forgotten, and they were brought out because of the motivation.

Creativity Makes a Difference

How can we use creativity in any area of life? Let me share with you one of the most exciting letters that I've gotten in a long, long time. It's from a man named Carl Hugebeck. He teaches character education, the "I CAN" course, down in Bastrop, Texas.

They had just finished the class, and here's what he said: "These kids are at risk. I reminded them that because they live in the United States of America, and lifelong education and self-improvement is a reality. Remember, Mr. Ziglar, these are at-risk students." Now we get into the creativity. "They have had difficult backgrounds and live in some deplorable situations. They are not supposed to be optimistic, enthusiastic, and goal-oriented—but they are. I tell them that they are 'at risk.' If they keep doing what they are doing, they will be 'at risk' of graduating, going to college, meeting their ideal mate, prospering, and enjoying the type of life God intended them to have. So, yes, thanks to character education and 'I CAN,' our students really are 'at risk!'"

Don't you just love that little twist there? Think of all the at-risk students who've been told over and over, "You're at risk! You're at risk! You're at risk! You've been a victim of this and that and the other." Of course, in many cases they are right—they *have* been victimized. However, doesn't it make more sense now to use that creative imagination and say, "You keep doin' this, you're 'at risk' of getting a promotion!" "You're 'at risk' of graduating." "You're at risk of being successful." "You're at risk of having lots of friends." Creativity makes a difference.

Let me give you another example here. Walter Williams just so happens to be one of my favorite economists. He regularly has columns in the *Dallas Morning News*, and a couple of weeks ago, he had an editorial in the *Dallas Morning News*. He explains that, "Anyim Palmer founded the Marcus Garvey School in South Central LA in '75. If you visited, you would see two-year-olds reciting the ABCs, three-year-olds counting in English, Spanish, and Swahili, and four-year-olds doing math. Down the hall, you would see second-graders spelling words like 'pharmaceutical,' 'entrepreneur,' and 'cerebellum,' and repeating The Gettysburg Address verbatim from memory."

What kind of school is it? It's not a rich, white, suburban school. It is a black school with four hundred students located in a troubled section of Los Angeles. Its students are not "gifted." They're ordinary kids with concerned parents. It's an ordinary school with black administrators and teachers who have unbounded pride and a sense of mission. Are the teachers real experts? No. They're regular teachers. As a matter of fact, they don't even have teaching credentials! Then what makes them so unique? They're given the freedom to adjust and be held accountable to teach the kids what is the most effective thing—what that student's needs are.

Now, what am I saying with all of this? I am saying that with creativity, we can do an awful lot more things.

Change Your Thinking

I'm going to share a little bit of information here that I just acquired. I'm enormously excited about it because there are a lot of people in our society who have behavior which is uncharacteristic or behavior which we cannot even begin to understand. So, as you read this, I want you to remember that what you get out of this book is not as important as what the book gets out of you.

I received a letter from a gentleman down in Florida named Leland M. Heller, M.D. He was talking about borderline disorder, "which affects between four and eight percent of the population and is one of the major preventable causes of child abuse, divorces, substance abuse and impulsive, violent crimes. It's a very important topic and a treatable illness. It's basically a form of epilepsy in the brain's limbic system. Victims have abnormal neurological examinations, brain waves, memory, and sleep. Borderline is clearly a medical problem, but it's also an emotion problem. Borderlines have no self-esteem, no effective psychological defenses, and have spent a lifetime with crippling mood swings, horribly painful dysphoria, and frequent bouts of psychosis, and have distorted their understanding of life and people."

This is the crux of my message. "Until the proper medication came along, they had essentially no chance to recover, even with counseling." This is where we need to understand people a little better. He points out that, "Somewhere between seven and twenty million people suffer from this disorder."

Now, where does this fit in your life? Well, he says, "In my opinion, it is unlikely a borderline will ever achieve mental wellness without reading positive books. They are as important as the drugs. Motivational audios are a must. Your car and the audio player can be the best school in the world. The more you listen, the healthier you become. Listen while getting dressed, cleaning the house, doing dishes, cooking, and so forth. You need the right information to change the way you think and feel."

Yesterday I had a conversation with Dr. Les Carter, who is on the staff at Minirth-Meier. I said, "Dr. Carter, I have an idea. Let me see what you think about it. In my opinion, the purpose of all counseling is to change your thinking."

"Zig, you are 100 percent on the target."

Changing the thinking of these people is making a dramatic difference. He had some nice things to say about me, but the following statements just about brought a tear to my eye.

"Zig is not only funny and motivational, but he describes values and attitudes that improve one's chances for a successful life. Untreated borderlines have shifting values due to their illness."

That happens to a lot of us, doesn't it? Shifting values?

> **Change your thinking and it will change your future.**

"Zig gives a set of values borderlines (and the rest of us) can believe in and live by. You may disagree with some things; not everyone agrees on everything Zig says (especially religion), but you will find few areas of disagreement. I greatly admire what his audio programs have done for my patients."

I recognize that sounds a little self-serving. Please forgive me if it does. Let me just say that what I want to do is communicate that when you have the right input—when that input is good and clean and pure and positive—what has happened in the past can change, without a shadow of a doubt. You change the future by changing your thinking; you change your thinking by putting the right things in your mind.

Do you believe that role models are important in life? Role models are enormously important! Do you believe the lifestyle of the role model will have an effect on the lifestyle of the person who emulates that role model? Let me tell you who the role models are of children in America who are between the ages of seven and twelve years old. Thirty-nine percent of them, their number one hero is a movie star or a television star. Nineteen percent of them, their hero is a singer. Eleven percent of them, their number one hero is a comedian, and eleven percent of them, their number one hero is an athlete.

I want you to search your memory bank, because I'm not putting down all of those people, but how many of them would you want your child to be like? To emulate? To follow their habits, their patterns, and so forth? In other words, we need to look at what we are putting in our minds. You see, a major business in today's world is counseling. Again, talking with Dr. Les Carter yesterday, I said, "Dr. Carter, what percentage of counseling has to do with relationships?"

He said, "One hundred percent of all counseling has to do, directly or indirectly, with relationships of one kind or another."

What's the most important relationship of all? The relationship you have with yourself. When you get along with you, it's easier to get along with somebody else. One recent survey revealed that when managers were asked about the most desirable trait they found in employees, eighty-four percent of them said, "I want somebody who can get along, be a part of the team, work with and cooperate with the rest of us."

How many of you have noticed that when you've got one wet blanket in the crowd, it puts a damper on the rest of them? When one negative person gets talking, it catches on, and that's why these managers are saying, "I want people who can get along with others."

The Power of Visualization

Many years ago, Marcus Aurelius said, "The happiness of your life depends upon the quality of your thoughts." What affects your thoughts? What goes in your mind? As I talked about a little bit earlier, your associates also affect your thoughts. Now, let me say that these principles that we're talking about work for individuals, they work for schools, they work for businesses, and they work for nations.

Suppose, just suppose, that these principles were taught. Now, let me clarify: I said *principles*, not always procedures, because when you try to get everybody following the same procedure, you've got some problems, haven't you? That stifles creativity. But you start with a base to build on, and that's what I'm talking about when I say *principles*.

I want to share with you a story which I believe represents our philosophy as well as any story I've ever heard. It involves an awful lot of these principles. As I share this story with you, I believe you're going to be thinking along the way, *Man alive, that ought to give **anybody** hope that they can do things in their life!*

In 1965, I gave my first major presentation when I was speaking in Kansas City on a program with Elmer Wheeler, Dr. Kenneth McFarland, Senator Milward Simpson, and Joe Batten. There were a bunch of heavy hitters at this presentation. I was the *new kid on the block*. I felt somewhat like the farmer who entered his mule in the Kentucky Derby. Somebody asked him, "You don't really think that mule's gonna fit in that derby, do you?"

He said, "Man, no! No way!"

"Well, why on Earth would you enter him?"

"Well, I just figure the association would be good for him."

You know, a lot of times we need association. Well, that was the role I was in, and when the seminar finished that evening, I headed back over to the Muelebach Hotel for what I thought was going to be a lonely dinner. I stepped out of the elevator, and I heard the booming voice of a man whom I now love as one of my closest friends, Bernie Lofchick, say to me, "Zig! Where're ya' goin'?"

I said, "Well, Bernie, I'm goin' to dinner."

He said, "Man, come to dinner with me and I'll buy!"

Well, that's one of those offers that's hard to refuse and, you know, people are happy when they can do things for you, and I like to make them happy.

"Brother Bern, you got a deal!"

We sat down to dinner and had instant rapport. We could relate on many things; we are both from large families; his dad died when he was young, he worked in a grocery store early on, I worked in a grocery store; he was the owner of the biggest cookware company in Canada, I'd sold cookware. So, we had a lot in common.

"Bernie, did you fly all the way down from Winnipeg to attend this seminar?"

He said, "Man, yeah! And was it ever worth it! I got some great ideas!"

"But Bernie! To come down from Winnipeg to here, that cost you a whole lot 'a money!"

"Yeah, Zig, but thanks to my son David, money is no problem for me."

"Brother Bern, that sounds like a story! Tell me."

"Well, when David was born, our joy was absolute and complete. We already had our two daughters, and now we had our son. But very quickly we came to know or realize that something was wrong. His little head hung too limply to the right side of his body. He drooled too much to be a normal, healthy child. We took him to the doctor, and he said, 'No problem. He's going outgrow it.' But deep down, we knew something was wrong. We took him to a specialist, and the specialist—one of the most respected ones in Canada—said, 'Well, he just has a reverse of club feet.' And for about six weeks they treated him for that. But we knew it was more serious. We took him to yet another specialist. After a very comprehensive examination, the specialist said, 'This little boy is a spastic. He has cerebral palsy. He's never going to be able to walk or talk or count to ten. I encourage you to put him in an institution for his own good, and for the good of the other members of the family.'"

Bernie Lofchick has the most alive eyes I've ever seen in my life. Those dark eyes were flashing wildly as he spoke.

"But, Zig, I'm not a buyer. I'm a seller. I could not see my son as a helpless, hopeless vegetable all of his life. I saw my son ..." (now here is his visualization we've talked about previously) "... as a happy, healthy, productive individual, so we went to another specialist, and another, and another. Over twenty specialists said, 'There is no hope for this boy.' Then we heard of a Dr. Perlstein down in Chicago, reputed to be the number one authority in the world on cerebral palsy, but he was so busy we could not get an appointment for the next two years."

Bernie is a salesman. He made some calls and connections. He learned that Dr. Perlstein was a bridge player and played with his son every Friday night. So, he got the son's phone number. He called and talked to Dr. Perlstein directly and made arrangements. Dr. Perlstein said that at the first cancellation they would call Bernie and Elaine to bring David down to Chicago for the exam. About eleven days later, the call came through. A little boy from Australia had canceled. They took David to Chicago, and Dr. Perlstein started all the process over. He took new X-rays, brought in the number one authority in Chicago to read those X-rays, and he said, "Don't tell me anything. I don't want any opinion. All I want you to tell me is exactly what you see."

When the examination was over, Dr. Perlstein called the Lofchicks in, and he said to them, "Your little boy is a spastic. He has cerebral palsy. He's never going to be able to walk or talk or count to ten ... if you listen to the prophets of doom. But," he said, "I want you to know that I am not problem-conscious; I am solution conscious. I believe there is something you can do for your son, if you're willing to do your part."

The Lofchicks said, "Doctor, we will do anything. Name the price." At that particular point in his career, they could not afford a heavy financial burden. Dr. Perlstein said, "It is going to cost an awful lot of money. But far more important than that, it's going to take an awful lot of commitment and patience and discipline on your part. You're going to have to push this little boy beyond all human endurance. Then you're going to have to push him some more. You're going to have to work him until he falls. You will then need to pick him up and work him some more. You need to understand that there's going to be months, sometimes years, when you cannot visually see any progress at all, but you cannot stop. You've got to keep going; otherwise, he will regress. One other thing; don't ever let him take therapy where he can physically see another victim of cerebral palsy taking therapy, because instinctively and subconsciously he will pick up the awkward, inadvertent moves that they sometimes make. Make certain there's a blockade, so he does not see those things."

When Bernie and Elaine headed back to Winnipeg, Canada, for the first time in their son's life, they headed back with some hope. They felt that the Goliath of cerebral palsy now had an opponent in David with a legitimate chance to win this battle. They hired a physical therapist and a bodybuilder, and they went to work. It took many months for David even to move the length of his own body. It took him many, many more months to do much more. Then, one day, the therapist called Bernie in his office and said, "Come on home, Bernie. I believe David is ready for the supreme effort."

Bernie rushed home, and they were all down in the basement, in the little gymnasium they'd built. The therapist, the body-builder, several of the neighbors, the two big sisters; everybody was around as David was on that little mat. He was going to attempt to do a pushup.

As that little body rose into the air, the physical and emotional exertion was so great that his body was covered with perspiration. The mat appeared as if somebody had sprinkled water on it. It was an effort that we cannot today conceive of being as great as it was. But when that perfect pushup was completed, David, Mom, Dad, the therapist, the bodybuilder, and the neighbors all broke down and literally wept. These were the tears that clearly said, "Happiness is not pleasure. Happiness is victory."

One of the highlights of our life took place on October 23, 1971, when we flew to Winnipeg, Canada, to attend the bar mitzvah of little David Lofchick. As that boy walked tall and straight and strong to the front of the synagogue to take part in the ceremony that would move him into the manhood of his faith, the only concession to the disease was a slight dragging of the right foot—which was so slight you had to know about it in advance to even have seen it. At that time, David had run as much as five miles nonstop. He had done up to one thousand pushups in a single day. He was running the wheels off his third bicycle. David was skating on the neighborhood hockey team.

What's so amazing about all of that is the doctors had said, "He has no motor connection to the right side of his body. He will never be able to swim. He will never be able to skate. He will never be able to ride a bicycle."

I give you all the details in this particular story because I believe it's one of the most moving, inspiring, important stories that I have ever been privileged to participate in.

I want to look at what I believe is going to be the very foundation of the visualization process that we're going to be dealing with. As we look at that story, I'm going to elaborate in considerable detail as we go along. This is our *Stairway to the Top*. At the top of the stairs are those things we want—we want to be happy, healthy, reasonably prosperous, the whole ballgame. At the very bottom, we have the foundation stones upon which you build. Now, I've only listed a half-dozen there—these are just some of those qualities. But everything—and I do mean everything—quite literally begins with a base.

When Dr. Ken McFarland, who was one of my heroes; one of the greatest speakers I've ever heard, and former superintendent of education up in Topeka, Kansas, was a little guy in school, his teacher asked him, "Ken, how far do you want to go in life?"

Ken said, "As far as I can."

Then she pointed to the floor and said, "Ken, the ladder starts here."

I cannot stress enough how incredibly important your foundation is.

5

THE FOUNDATION
FOR GREATNESS

I know everybody has heard the *good news* / *bad news* stories a few thousand times. The progression is pretty consistent and most often goes like this: A fella came home, and his wife said, "Honey, I've got some good news and some bad news."

He said, "Well, what's the good news?"

She replies, "The airbags work."

I don't know how many of you ever have memory lapses or problems. I have a brilliant memory myself. It's just awful short!

I love the story of the two old codgers who were visiting, and one of them enthusiastically said, "You know, I've been to this new doctor, and he's given me this exciting new medicine! It's just helped my memory so much!"

"Well, what's the name of it?"

"I'm tryin' to remember... what is the name of that flower... the stem's long, and it's got thorns on it?"

"A rose."

"Yeah. Hey, Rose, what is the name of that ..."

A Serious Look at Values

Let's take a serious look at one of the lessons we can learn from the David Lofchick story. First of all, let's look at the foundation stone of honesty. When times are tough, and you've really got a difficult assignment in front of you, there are occasions when honesty is an absolute must. To tell somebody what they want to hear today, knowing that it's going to come back and bite you tomorrow, is destructive.

David's doctors, therapist, and family were honest with him. "Son, this is gonna keep going a long time." So, they prepared him for the long journey. Honesty is a tremendously important foundation stone to build on.

What is character? It's the ability to carry out a good resolution long after the excitement of the moment has passed. When we set those long-term goals, character is what's going to enable us to reach them, because there will be those times when we will want to quit. We wonder, *is it really worth it?* I think if you were to see David Lofchick today, you would say yes, it really is worth it.

David is 35 years old and has three beautiful children. The only concession he makes to the disease is so minute that you could not even identify it unless you knew about it. He's an entrepreneur and is enormously successful in the real estate business. He works with his dad in one of the largest Maytag distributorships in the world, and he has now opened his own computer store. He's got a lot of things going for him. Was the journey of healing worth it? I know he would say, "Absolutely. A thousand times yes, it was worth it."

His success was built on integrity. With integrity, you have nothing to fear because you have nothing to hide. Let me tell you what else this story is built on. It's built on love. It is one of the most beautiful love stories I think I've ever heard. When David was about eighteen months old, they had to put braces on those little legs.

> **With integrity, you have nothing to fear because you have nothing to hide.**

Every night when they put them on, they had to progressively get them tighter and tighter. He was a beautiful little boy. Green eyes, olive complexion, coal black hair. Every night, David would look at his mom or his dad and say to them, "Mom, do you have to put them on tonight?" "Do you have to make them so tight?"

I don't think there's a single parent who cannot relate to what I'm now saying. Your child, your baby, the one you love, with tears in his eyes, is saying, "Can't we leave them off tonight?" "Do you have to make them so tight?" But David's parents, Bernie and Elaine, loved him so much they were willing to say no to the tears of the moment so they could say yes to the healthy laughter of a lifetime. See, loving someone doesn't mean you always give them what they think they want at that moment. Loving someone is doing for that person what is best for that person at that moment. That's what love is all about.

Consider the loyalty of Bernie's family to David. The loyalty of the sisters, the loyalty of the therapist and the bodybuilder; they became an incredibly close family. You know, a lot of times serious illnesses split families apart. This one brought that family closer together.

So, Zig, how does this apply in the business world; in our own success? How important is loyalty? One afternoon several years ago, I was in my home writing. The doorbell rang, and I went to the door. It was a good friend of mine named Bryan Flanagan, who also worked with us. Bryan was a little pensive and a little hesitant as he came in. He said, "You know, I hate to interrupt what you're doing, but I just brought you some news and wanted to tell you personally." What he had come to tell me was that he was leaving the company. He said, "Let me tell you about an offer I've got, Zig, and I'm enormously excited about it." As he started describing it, I have to tell you, I got excited about his opportunity, too!

I said, "Well, Bryan, I gotta tell ya', I hate to see you go! I really do!" He was a very valuable member of our staff. But he left with my blessings.

He came back a few months later and said, "Well, everything that glitters is not gold. I would like to come back and work with you again." We were, of course, elated to have him back.

I want to tell you why he got that offer in the first place. Everywhere Bryan Flanagan went, he was talking about what a great company he worked for and about what a fine person I was. He was bragging about all the people down there. He was saying, "Man, it's a great place to work! The attitude is so great! Everybody tries to live like they say they do. It's a wonderful place to work!"

How many of you think Bryan would have gotten any job offer or opportunity from anybody else if everywhere he went he said, "Man, you can't believe that lousy, no-good outfit I work for! I mean, it's a bunch'a bums out there, they tell ya' one thing, do another thing. I can't understand anybody actin' like they do out there!" How many employers would have said, "Man, that sounds like the kinda guy I'd like to have workin' for me!" You see, loyalty is unquestionably practical. What I'm talking about here is something that is applicable in every area of life.

The man of character finds a special attractiveness in difficulty since it is only by coming to grips with difficulty that he can realize his potential. Many, many times, I wondered how much bigger, stronger, faster, and smarter David would have been if he was given all the chances at birth that you and I were given. Then, one day, it hit me like a ton of bricks. Had he been given more, he, in all probability, would have ended up with less. Maybe considerably less. That's one of the reasons I take refuge in my faith so often. You know, the Scripture says, "All things work together for good to them who love God." We're supposed to thank God for difficulties. The more I delve into the research I do, the more I become convinced that we develop those strengths by overcoming the difficulties we encounter in our life.

I have been accused, on occasion, of using some clichés, and I'm going to deal with that in just a moment. For now, I would like to emphasize how the principles I'm talking about can work in your personal life, your family life, your business life, and yes, these principles can even work nationally. You may have heard about Edwards Deming, the man who literally revolutionized the Japanese system of doing things. Homer Sarason was another one of those management gurus who went over there and did a tremendous job for them. I'm going to tell you why Deming, Sarason, and the other management and leadership experts who went to Japan were able to do the things that they were able to do.

Japan is a little nation that is about half the size of the state of Texas, and two-thirds of the land cannot be used for anything. They have no natural resources, no oil, no gas, no coal, no iron ore—none of those things. Japan has only half as many people as we have, and yet, they are the number one creditor nation in the entire world. Why? Because they have developed the resource which is the most important resource of all, and it ties into what Oliver Wendell Holmes said about each individual: "The great tragedy in America is not the waste of our natural resources, though that is great. The great tragedy is the waste of our human resources," because, "The average person goes to their grave with their music still in them."

It's a cliché, but you know it's true. You're the only one who can use your ability. It is an awesome responsibility.

Why were the Japanese able to do so much? It was because of what Douglas MacArthur did. What did he do? He knew that since 1870, when Matthew C. Perry opened the doors to Japan, that he could not change a war-like nation overnight into a peaceful, producing nation. He knew he had to start at the very base—with the children. He brought in an educator, Dr. Mark T. Ohr, to completely revive the educational structure in Japan.

Dr. Bill Kirby, who was commissioner of education in the state of Texas, went to Japan and did a study on the Japanese educational system. I, too, went to Japan because I wanted to see what was going on over there. Dr. Kirby's exploration was considerably more in-depth because he had better cooperation than a private citizen could get. Here is what they learned: In Japanese kindergarten, one hour a day, every day, they teach a course emphasizing the values of honesty, character, integrity, hard work, loyalty, thrift, enthusiasm, positive thinking, responsibility, patriotism, and free enterprise. What have we been talking about during this entire book? There is a relationship of cooperation between the parent and the student and between the educator and the government and the businesspeople; they all work together. What happened in Japan is they were turning out a workforce that was ready to go to work. That's what I'm talking about, developing a workforce built on the principles that we've been talking about throughout this book.

The Thomas Jefferson Center in Pasadena, California, spent years studying values, and here's what they found. There are fifteen values that are common in all the world's great civilizations and religions:

1. Wisdom
2. Integrity
3. Love
4. Freedom (that's where creativity is born)
5. Justice
6. Courage
7. Humility
8. Patience
9. Industriousness
10. Thriftiness
11. Generosity
12. Objectivity
13. Cooperation
14. Moderation
15. Optimism

These are the qualities we've identified from the very beginning.

Listen to what former President Ronald Reagan said about this, and I think he gets right to the heart of it, "If we fail to instruct our children in justice, religion, and liberty, we will be condemning them to a world without virtue, a life in the twilight of a civilization where the great truths have been forgotten." I believe he's right.

Attitude, ladies and gentlemen, can be good today and bad tomorrow. We know how things happen to us, and we react instead of respond, and so our attitude is subject to a lot of things. I read this by Milton Segal and thought it was neat. He said, "I'm a walking economy. A man was overheard to say one day, 'My hairline's in a recession, my waist is a victim of inflation, and together they're putting me in a deep depression.'"

The Little Things are Important

Attitude

Your attitude is important. In *The New York Times*, Daniel Goleman had an interesting article. This, again, ties right into the David Lofchick story. But, more importantly (as far as you are concerned) it ties into your story; it ties into your life. "A study of more than 2,800 men and women 65 and older found that those who rate their health 'poor' are 45 times more likely to die in the next four years than those who rate their health 'excellent.' This was the case even if examination showed the respondents to be in comparable health. You are drawn closer to the strongest picture in your mind, and the result, in this case, was fatal. These findings are supported by a review of five other large studies totaling 23,000 people."

The old saying, "As a man thinketh in his heart, so is he," has so much validity here. Whether you think you can or think you can't, you are absolutely right. When Bernie Lofchick got the news that his son was a spastic and would be a vegetable, he immediately said, "I don't buy that idea. I see my son living a happy, healthy, and normal life."

> **Whether you think you can or think you can't, you are absolutely right.**

A lot of faith is involved in a situation like that. I love the story of the fellow who stopped at the mountain overlook to get a better view of the scenery. He got a little too close to the edge, the foundation collapsed on him, and he started falling. There was about a 400-foot drop. He caught on to the last remaining little tree that was hanging there and started shouting for help.

Then there was a deep voice, "Son, do you believe?"

"Oh, yes! I believe! I believe!"

"Let go of the limb."

"Is there anybody else up there?"

Unfortunately, a lot of people are too often in that mode of faith.

Relationships

Let's look at another thing. In the beginning, David Lofchick could not have a good, healthy self-image. But Dr. Tony Campolo says your image is influenced by the most important person in your life more than anything else. Who were the most important people in his life? His parents. What did they do to reinforce that image? Every night, from when David was a baby until he got to be a teenager, Bernie Lofchick worked in a housewares company. For seven years, Bernie worked seven days and seven nights a week. He took one Friday night off in seven years. The reason he did it was because of the enormity of the expenses that went with giving David this chance in life.

In the process, he became the largest housewares distributor in Canada, and he got there simply because he was helping his son get what he wanted out of life.

Was it tough? It sure was. But every night when Bernie would come in, David would be asleep. He would awaken him, hold him in his arms, and say, "Son, I love you very much. I want you to know that you can do anything you really want to do, son. You are a winner in every sense of the word."

His wife, Elaine, had already told David that before he went to sleep the first time, but over and over, the love was total, it was unconditional, and he grew up with that security. Security—or your image, rather—is so enormously important.

In building relationships, let's look at the Stairway to the Top. You'll see that at the top, we look at what you want. At the bottom, we look at the foundation, and then we take the steps in order to get there. The elevator to the top is out of order. It always has been. You have to take the stairs, and you have to take them one at a time.

Relationships are so important. All these things are important. What's the most important? I do not know. But, I can tell you this: It begins with having the right attitude. The right attitude about the way you see yourself. The right attitude toward your fellow human being. The right attitude toward your job. The right attitude toward the company you work with. The right attitude toward the community you live in. The right attitude toward the country of which we are a part. All of it becomes important.

When talking about love relationships in the family, let me make a little confession to you. I have three daughters and a son. There has never been a doubt in my mind that I love each of my children equally. However, I noticed something that was happening in my life. As my son grew into a man, got married, and went into business for himself, I started noticing something that I never would have noticed had I not heard what Bill Glass had to say, and that simply is this: "I never see one of my girls, I never talk to them on the telephone, that somewhere in the conversation I don't tell them how much I love them. Now, I love my boy fully as much as I do my girls, but over the years, I'd kinda gotten away from telling him. You know, us men, sometimes we don't 'say' those things."

I heard Bill Glass talk about an experience with his 285-pound son. He hugged him and said, "Son, I sure love you." His son said, "Thanks, Dad. I needed that!" Everybody needs that. You know, the sad thing is so many of us love our family so much, but somehow or another we expect them to just figure it out by osmosis. I'm telling you, it needs to be verbalized. Two days after I'd heard Bill Glass, my son and I had a round of golf, which is our favorite recreational activity. When we got back to the house, we were moving the clubs from my car over to his, and I said, "Son, you know, I've got a confession to make to you. I've noticed over a period of time that I've neglected something which is extraordinarily important. I have just about quit telling you how much I love you, and I want you to know, son, that I do love you."

My son said, "Well, Dad, I know that." But there was just a trace of a tear as he grabbed me and gave me a hug. Ever since then, when we greet each other, it is no longer with a handshake. He gives me a hug. Dads, I can't say it strongly enough. Moms are going to do it, but dads, it's so important that you hug your sons. I don't care if he's 28 years old or 65 years old. You need to hug that son of yours. I know you're going to hug your girls, but you need to hug your boy and tell him that you love him. That makes all the difference in the world.

I believe that one of the prime reasons David has done so well is because he was given that reassurance over and over and over. One of the reasons that out of 40,000 people in the jails of Florida, only 13 of them are Jews is because it goes back to Abraham, Isaac, and Jacob, where the Jewish father would say, "Bless you, my son," and "I love you, son," and they would give them that big hug.

Achievable Goals

David obviously had big goals. His dad set them initially. They were long-range goals; he was going to be a normal, happy, and healthy boy. However, he also had to have daily goals. So, in the process of growing up, he had financial goals, academic goals, sales goals, athletic goals—whatever your goals might be, they're all woven together. You need a *series* of goals in life. Sometimes, when the goal is so long, maybe we lose just a little bit of sight of the final objective unless we have those daily objectives along the way.

One of my favorite people in life is Byron Nelson, and I share this with you because it supports exactly what I'm talking about. Byron, in 1944, won eight golf tournaments and $38,000—that was a lot of money on the golf tour in those days! Heck, it was a lot of money in life in those days! Now, that got him set for 1945. In 1945, he set a record which will never be broken—I emphatically believe that. Nobody will ever approach the record he established in 1945. He won eleven consecutive golf tournaments. He entered thirty-one tournaments and won a total of eighteen before the year was over. He placed second seven times.

Twenty-five out of thirty-one were no worse than second. The worst he ever finished was ninth.

What set up 1945 was 1944. What sets up a winner is what you do before you get to that critical moment. Winning those tournaments in 1944 set the stage. But let me tell you what was really responsible. He was keeping exact records.

"You know, I was so consistent in my game I could hit the fairway just about every shot, hit the green on my second or third shot, I'd sink the putt, I'd get my birdie or get a par, and frankly, it got a little boring!" What Byron did was he remembered that his long-range goal and his big goal was to buy a ranch. His financial goal was to pay cash for it. Now, fortunately, he kept exact records on every round in 1944. He knew exactly how he hit each drive, how he hit each chip, each putt, each iron shot. He knew exactly how he'd hit every single shot, period. And in the process, he noticed two things. He noticed, first of all, his lack of concentration, because it had now gotten boring to him. He also noticed that the shot he was missing the most was the chipping. He never would have known those things if he had not kept those records.

Desire to Succeed

In 1945, Byron started identifying things. He would say, "Well, now, if I can chip this in, that'll help me buy another cow. If I win this tournament, I can buy another ten acres of land," and he literally identified each thing and tied them together. What I'm saying here is look at the lessons we can glean from David and Byron. David had goals of increasing his number of pushups, sit-ups, and the distance he ran. He was willing, as you will see, to work very, very hard at that. Byron was willing to work hard at keeping records, identifying and achieving his next goal and shot.

For example, for one solid winter—remember, here's a guy who had no sense of balance—every morning, David set his opportunity clock one hour earlier than any other member of the family. He'd wake up, he'd get his ice skates on, and he would crawl out to the frozen swimming pool every morning one solid winter just to learn how to stand up. How did he learn how to ride a bicycle? Well, they hired a physical therapist, and David would get on the bike and the therapist would run behind him, literally stabilizing it until David could learn to maneuver himself without having any sense of balance. He tore up a couple of bicycles before he was able to learn to do it. He injured himself, scratched his knee a number of times, and some kids were awfully cruel on occasion. Kids would run out at David, knowing he would have to swerve to miss them and without that sense of balance, down he would go. Those were discouraging times. What would David do? He'd get right back up and he'd get to it. He wanted to succeed.

A lot of folks are not going to be nice to us as we go through life. In fact, a lot of times, they're going to get in our way. You have to *want to* succeed. This thing called desire is incredibly important.

You might say, "But, Zig, lemme tell you about that son of mine," or "that daughter of mine." Or, "Lemme tell you about some of the workers! They don't really have any desire. They're content to go through life in mediocrity. I do everything I can; I cannot get them inspired!"

> **Desire changes the hot water of mediocrity to the steam of outstanding success.**

Why is desire so important? Desire is what changes the hot water of mediocrity to the steam of outstanding success. Little things do make big differences in life. It's the part of the blanket that hangs over the bed that keeps you warm.

How many sales managers have ever had a salesperson come to them and say, "Hey, don't give me full commission on this one, I just barely made it, half commission would be OK"? You see, what I'm saying is the difference between success and failure is frequently measured in minute amounts.

Suppose people still say, "I don't wanna do it!" A lot of people who say they don't want to are really saying, "I don't believe I can. The picture I have of myself is that of a loser." So, what we've got to do is work on their confidence and their self-esteem. Convince them that they can, and desire will be born.

I read the newspaper every day. Now, a lot of times, people say, "Well, I avoid the newspaper; it is full of bad news!" I'm here to tell you, folks, you can find whatever you look for. For ten years, I taught a large Sunday school class 48 weeks out of the year. I always started that class by reading the newspaper to the class. I would read them the good news they might have missed that week. I can absolutely guarantee you that in any newspaper in America, of any city size, I can find something in it that is optimistic and upbeat, and I can use it that day in my life. It just depends on what you're looking for.

Influence

A lot of people find fault like there is a reward for it. We need to start looking for some of the good things. There was a beautiful article in the *Dallas Morning News*. The columnist, Steve Blow, was writing about Tony Casillas, who was a big tackle for the Dallas Cowboys. He had been over to Dallas Sunset High School and had told the kids, "The eight of you who have the most improvement in attendance and the most improvement in your grades, I'm gonna take you out to dinner."

The competition was really tough. One of the winners was Israel Ramirez. Now, Israel was an interesting young man. He was making Ds and Fs on his grades. He got involved in this competition and ended up on the honor roll. As he put it, one of the things that happened along the way was changing his friends. The friends he'd been running with were Ds and Fs and dropouts, so he changed his friends. The *LA Times* did an extensive article and said that, "People who go to the top, invariably, at one time in their life make a conscious decision to associate with winners instead of losers." You know the Bible says, "Be not deceived. Evil companions corrupt good morals." I can tell you, having worked in the drug war an awfully long time, that if a youngster is running with kids who are doing drugs, the odds are eight times as great that he or she is going to get involved in drugs. That's the power of peer pressure.

In Deuteronomy 20:8, God says if some of these guys don't want to fight, if they have a spirit of fear, send them home because they will pollute and influence the others. That'll make them scared, and then we will end up losing the battle. Be sure to associate with the right people.

Another of the winners was a young man named Raymond Sanchez. Now, Raymond had been taught right; his mom had brought him up with the right principles. When he moved to the eighth grade, he changed schools, and, incidentally, parents, when your child changes schools, many times it's a bigger school. They've got to make new friends and many times the kids who are involved in sexual activity, gangs, thievery and this sort of thing, simply look upon them as *fresh meat*. These gangs zero in on them, and a lot of times a child wants to be accepted by just about anybody. Moving into a new school can be a huge danger zone. That's where we really need to keep our eyes open.

When Raymond went to this new school, he noticed there was an eighth-grader there who literally ran the school. He was pretty cool, and also in charge of drugs there. Raymond started dressing like him, cutting his hair like him, walking like him, and talking like him. Soon Raymond was selling drugs. It started out as selling pot. It later moved to cocaine and Corvettes. At one time, there were many people in his gang. Soon the drive-by shootings started, and he realized things were not going well.

When you look at influence, it works both ways. His girlfriend was going to Dallas Can Academy. She was telling him, "Raymond, this is a wonderful school! I'm learning some tremendous things!" So he decided to get into that school. It consists entirely of dropouts and kids who are in trouble. His girlfriend influenced him for the good. The bottom line is that he realized after he'd been there a couple of days that his life was miserable. He had money, cars, girls and everything else, but he realized his life was going nowhere fast, so he bought into another idea.

He graduated as the valedictorian of his class. The City of Dallas hired him into its Gang Intervention Program, and today, he's working with Dallas Can! Grant East, who runs the Academy, said that he really is a unique young man.

Now, what other message am I delivering? I'm simply saying this. It's too soon to ever give up on our kids. Sometimes it's tempting. But you have to resist. Along those same lines, it's too soon to ever give up on yourself.

Change Your Picture

Let me remind you again if you've forgotten: Failure is an event—it is not a person. Yesterday ended last night, and today really is a new day. When I was 45 years old, I was stone broke and in debt. I had worked all of my life and had a good attitude, but until I bought into the idea of these principles and changing this picture I had of myself, the changes were not going to happen. They only did once I changed that picture.

These young people changed. But what I'm also saying is that the values we have are of utmost importance. We're getting to that point where there are so very few moral absolutes. One of my salespeople, Don Michael, had a rather interesting phone conversation. A teacher called and was talking to him about some of the products we sell. Don was saying, "Here is what this teaches."

"We can't use that; we cannot teach the kids what is right and what is wrong."

"Wait a minute. You can't tell them what's right and wrong?"

"No, that's judgmental and, you know, we simply present the facts. We can't tell them what's right and what's wrong."

"I'm a little puzzled now. You can't tell them what's wrong, but if they do wrong, we put them in jail. Is that fair?"

Morals

Morals are important. Now, a lot of times people say, "You talk about values. Whose values?" I have a list that I use to challenge parents, educators, and well, just about anybody. "Go down the list and tell me which one do you not want your child to be taught. Do you not want him to be taught honesty? How about character? How about responsibility? Disobedience? Is that OK?

How about commitment and enthusiasm and a positive mental attitude?"

I am not talking religion. After 200 years of teaching faith in our schools, we can't do that anymore. What I am talking about is values, and what you're talking about here is values. In our "I CAN" Course we don't teach religion, but we do teach the values.

I believe John F. Kennedy expressed it quite well. This is an excerpt from a speech he would have made here in Dallas:

> "We in this country and this generation are by destiny, rather than by choice, the watchmen of the walls of world freedom. We ask, therefore, that we may be worthy of the power and the responsibility that we may exercise our strength with wisdom and restraint, that we may achieve in our time and for all times the ancient vision of peace on Earth, goodwill toward men. That must always be our goal, and the righteousness of our call must always underlie our strength. For as it was written long ago, 'Except the Lord keep the city, the watchman waketh but in vain.'"

I agree. These values are what built our country. We're a values-oriented society. How many of you would prefer to have somebody who was honest and worked hard and was enthusiastic? Isn't that a silly question? Yet it's one that has to be answered.

This is one of my favorite stories along these lines… many, many years ago, a wise old king called all his wise men together. Once they were huddled around, he said, "I want you to compound for me the wisdom of the ages. I want you to put it in bound book form." They went out and they wrote for a long time. They came back with twelve huge volumes. The king looked at them, and he said, "I'm sure this is the wisdom of the ages, but hey, it's too lengthy! People won't read it. You have got to condense it."

They came back with just one volume, then a chapter, then a page, and finally they came back with a paragraph. Ultimately, they came back with one sentence because the king kept telling them, "Condense it. Condense it. Condense it." When he looked at that one sentence, the king said, "Hey! That's it! As soon as all men everywhere learn this, then most of our problems will be solved." The sentence simply said, *"There ain't no free lunch!"*

Folks, that's an important message. There really ain't no free lunch. We do have to work. The successful family has work as the father and integrity as the mother. Get along with the parents, and you won't have any trouble with the rest of the family.

Hard Work

Work is the foundation of all business, the source of all prosperity, and the parent of genius. Work can do more to advance youth than his own parents, be they ever so wealthy. It is represented in the humblest savings and has laid the foundation of every fortune. It is the salt that gives life its savor, but it must be loved before it can bestow the greatest blessing and achieve its greatest ends. When loved, work makes life sweet, purposeful, and fruitful.

> **Work is the foundation of business, the source of prosperity, and the parent of genius.**

I know, I'm dealing in a lot of clichés. Let me share something. Some people are quick to condemn clichés. But what is a cliché? It is a truth that has retained its validity through time. Mankind would lose half its hard-earned wisdom, built up patiently over the ages, if it ever lost its clichés.

Here's another little one: There aren't any hard and fast rules for getting ahead in the world—just hard ones.

Is success easy? Is anything easy? No, but it can be fun, and that's the thing we're trying to emphasize. The most practical, beautiful philosophy in all the world won't work if you won't. Education covers a lot of ground, but it won't cultivate any of it.

One of my favorite stories has to do with something that happened many, many years ago. It was a hot day out in the Midwest, and a work crew was working on a section of the railroad when this luxury railroad car rolled by, and the last one was this gorgeous luxury caboose. They recognized it immediately for what it was. The window opened on that last luxury car, and a voice called out,

"Dave! Is that you, Dave Anderson? Over here!"

Dave Anderson was leading that work crew in the hot sun, and Jim Murphy was the voice calling.

"Come on over, Dave, I wanna talk to ya'!" Dave was very happy to get out of that hot sun into that air-conditioned car, and so he walked over and he and Jim greeted each other warmly outside. They went in, they had a marvelous visit for about an hour, and Dave got ready to go back out to the crew. Again, he and Jim shook hands warmly and talked another minute out there, and then Dave went back to his work crew.

One of the workers asked, "Dave? Do you know who that is?"

"Why, sure! It's Jim Murphy. President of the railroad!"

"How do you know Jim Murphy so well?"

"Over 20 years ago he and I went to work for this railroad on the same day."

"How do you explain this, Dave? You are still out here workin' in the sun, and he is in an air-conditioned car and named president of the railroad."

Dave Anderson's answer is one of the great lessons of life.

"Over 20 years ago, I went to work for a dollar and seventy-five cents an hour. Jim Murphy went to work for the railroad."

It's a two-way street. You see, the company needs to provide training, inspiration, and opportunity. When the worker provides excitement, enthusiasm, commitment, and honest effort; that simply means that both of them, management and workers, are on the same side. When that happens, productivity will no longer be a problem.

Teamwork

The Redhead and I had an opportunity to see the musical *Crazy for You*. We were absolutely enthralled with that particular presentation. I almost never see anything that I don't start thinking, "Now, how can I use this? What am I learnin'?" That's where I get my greatest enjoyment. As I watched those 27 or 28 performers out there, I was absolutely fascinated! As I looked at them, I thought, "There are some lessons that we can learn from this." Number one, the effort that every singer and dancer was expending was total. I mean, they really gave it their all. They were giving their all at the end just as much as they were at the very beginning. Their enthusiasm for what they were doing was completely contagious. They had a conviction that their role made the difference in whether it was going to be a successful presentation or not. Do you know what? They were right!

It's the same old story: "For the want of a nail the shoe was lost, for want of the shoe the horse was lost, for want of the horse the rider was lost, for want of the rider the battle was lost, for want of the battle the country was lost." Many times, one person breaks down; and particularly in small companies, that does create a lot of problems.

I wish you could have seen the commitment on that stage. I mean, these guys and gals, they were committed to doing their absolute best. They were giving it their all. What intrigued me most was how you could just feel and see the way they were encouraging each other. As if to say, "Come on!" "You can do it! You can do it!" When one would be singing, the others would be looking at them, and you could just feel that they were encouraging one another. Just think about what that kind of attitude would do in the culture of most companies. Their team spirit was absolutely beautiful. They knew they were functioning as one. I've got to tell you; there was a lot of trust involved.

I don't know if you've ever really watched active dancers or not, but I'm telling you, you've got to be in good physical shape. You've got to be an athlete to do a lot of those things. The intriguing thing for me was that here is the star of the show, who was doing all this cavorting all over the place, and for five minutes, he never even looked behind him. Then he came up and there was a collapse, a big drop-off behind him, and without even glancing behind, back he went! Now, if somebody were not there to catch him, he would have been seriously injured. He had to trust that there was because of all the things that had happened before. That also brings up the awe of the timing that is involved. You see, the timing of what we do is important. But most of all, they were having fun. I mean, they were having an enormously good time in doing what they were doing. When you can have some fun in what you're doing, I believe that whatever the job is, we all can get some enjoyment out of it somewhere along the way.

Humor

There's a bit of humor in almost everything that happens. I know this is going to sound like cruel humor, but he laughed the loudest himself (after he got through crying). Jim Norman, the CEO of our company, was walking into the offices one day, and it was slippery right there in front of the building. He slipped, and he ended up flat-out on the ground. About half the people saw him there, and they just thought that was the funniest thing ever. Now, obviously, he was not hurt, or they would not have been laughing.

So, what's funny about seeing somebody fall? How many of you have ever fallen? Don't you feel the absolute silliest you've ever felt in your life? If it doesn't hurt, that is! I mean, you're just so embarrassed. It happened to me here a couple of weeks ago. We were riding in the tram out at Dallas/Fort Worth airport, and they always say, "hold onto something." Shoot, I know everything's going to be alright, so I'm just standing there, and all of a sudden, bam! I mean, they put the brakes on that thing, and I went tumbling down like a ton of bricks. After I got over the shock and a little embarrassment and discovered I was not hurt, then I thought it was funny, too. You can have some fun at it!

Discover, Develop and Motivate Yourself

These guys and gals in this *Crazy for You* musical were hard workers. I mean, they were giving it their all. Put that to work in your personal life, in your school, in your family, and in your company. You'll be amazed at what the results are going to be.

Let me tell you the rest of the story. There probably isn't more than ten percent of people reading this who are not making more money than everybody in that production except maybe the top three or four people. It's one of the most uncertain industries in all the world.

Why do they do it? First of all, they love to do it. Second, every one of them has a conviction deep down that someday they are going to "make it big." The odds are astronomical that they won't, but without that hope, there is not going to be any chance at all. What I'm really saying is that in whatever it is that you do, the odds are considerably higher that with the same effort, the same commitment, the same enthusiasm, the same commitment to rehearsing again, over and over, that what you do off the job is the determining factor in how far you go on the job. You prepare before you go to work.

But, here's a major point I want to make. When it was all over, if there had been no applause for all that effort, then that play, that musical, would have died long ago. Shakespeare said that the applause of a single human being is of great consequence. All of us need applause. My friend James Howard, who is a consultant at our company, does motion studies and productivity studies. In answer to the question, "What does management say when you complete a task?" his reply is seen in the following statistic. Ninety-four percent of them said, "Management says nothing." Think of what a downer that is! Apply this and we can get so much more done in our lives.

This question often comes up: Why is it that people do not develop their talent and work as hard as they're capable of working and doing? Denial is the first thing. You see, if you deny you have the ability and the talent, then that gives you that loser's limp, that excuse: "Well, you can't expect much of me, 'cause I haven't got much!" That's the reason so much of this book has been dedicated to changing that picture you have of yourself.

Here is another one of my favorite stories ... at turn of the century, down in Beaumont, Texas, a man was selling his property, bit by bit, because there was a depression and a drought. An oil company came along and said, "Sir, we think there's oil underneath your property. Let us drill for oil. If we discover it, we will pay you royalties on every barrel."

Well, the man had nothing to lose, and a great deal to gain. He said, "Let's do it." So they drilled for the oil. In those days, the derricks were made out of wood. When they brought in a gusher, the force of the gusher destroyed the derrick. The greater the destruction, the greater the excitement. When this one came in, it blew the derrick to smithereens, and for the next eleven days, hundreds of thousands of barrels of oil poured out before they could put the cap on it. It was Spindletop, the most significant, productive single oil well in history. Three major oil companies were born out of that field that day. The man became an instant millionaire. Or did he?

> **Your abilities have value if you recognize, claim and develop them.**

You see, in reality, he'd been a millionaire many times over ever since he had acquired the property. However, until they discovered the oil, brought it to the surface, took it to the marketplace, and cashed it in, it had no value. You see, it doesn't make any difference how much ability you have. Unless you recognize that ability and confess that ability (you thought "confession" was a dirty word, didn't you?) and then develop that ability, it really does not have value.

That's what this book really is all about. It's about discovering and then developing yourself. It's about motivating yourself. A lot of people never get started; they're procrastinators. Tomorrow is the greatest labor-saving device ever invented. That is why a lot of people never do things. They're *going to*, but not today.

There is that fear of failure that I talked about in the goal-setting segment. What is fear? Remember, it forms an acrostic for *False Evidence Appearing Real.*

The next reason a lot of people don't get in it is they are self-centered and irresponsible. You know, "That's not my deal!" You know, "I'm thinkin' … here's what I wanna do, I wanna do my thing!" They never accept the responsibility for using their own ability. They're deeply involved in the blame game. They blame somebody else, or they blame society. They blame everybody without looking at themselves.

A lot of them say, "I deserve better than that." Isn't that something? "I deserve better than that." "I want to start at the top!" The only people who really start at the top are grave diggers, and as you know, they end up in the hole!

I've previously talked about immigrants, how they have four times as good a chance of becoming a millionaire as do native-born Americans. The reason they do is because when they come into America, as I stated earlier, they're gung-ho about taking a minimum wage job because minimum wage for them is maximum wage where they came from. They don't look for the better opportunity; they look for the opportunity and make it better. There's the difference, right there.

6

OVERCOMING ADVERSITY
TO LIVE YOUR DREAMS

One night at about eleven o'clock in an empty fast-food restaurant, the chairman of the board came walking in. He looked around and didn't see anybody at the counter, but he could see a guy in the back smoking a cigarette. Oh, he about hit the ceiling! He went charging around the counter, and not only was the clerk who was supposed to be up front smoking a cigarette, but the manager was sitting back there, also smoking a cigarette.

Well, the chairman read them the riot act. I mean, he tore that guy apart all up and down, and the manager was pretty cool about it. Finally, when the chairman had finished reaming him out, the manager said, "And just who are you?"

The guy said, "I'm the chairman of the board of this company. Now, what do you think about that?"

The guy was very cool. He replied, "I think you and I are both about as high in this organization as we're ever gonna go!"

I get so irritated when I hear this expression on the news, and by celebrities and athletes, "You'll end up flippin' hamburgers in a fast-food restaurant."

Hamburger Flipper to CEO

I want to talk about the hamburger flippers of life, because I happen to believe that any work that is honest, that is productive, that does a service, is a good job. Let me make some observations as we look at some of those hamburger flippers.

First of all, it teaches the youngsters discipline and responsibility. That is not all bad. Second, it teaches them pride in performance. Many of them, for the first time, learn the importance of personal grooming, being neatly dressed, and being dependable. They learn the value of money and thrift when they start buying things themselves and discover that their money will not buy everything in sight. I've been so amazed at a study done in California with high-school dropouts. They would interview them and ask, "Now, what are you gonna do?"

They'd say, "Well, I'm gonna get me a job. I'm gonna rent me a little apartment. Then I'm gonna get me a car." They start enumerating the things they want, but the bottom line is they cannot even get close to earning as much money as is required to have all those things.

Now, think of the advantage if that youngster had been working ten or twelve hours a week on a part-time basis and learned just exactly what they can buy with that money. As a youngster, I worked in a grocery store in Yazoo City, Mississippi. I was a teller in that store. I am not trying to impress you with the title; it just meant that I told people to move while I swept.

In the summer months, our business was awfully slow. I remember so vividly the day the boss was trying to get all of us busy, and there was nothing to do. He said, "Why don't you all get busy?"

I said, "Well, Mr. Anderson, whatcha want me to do?"

"Well, you can dust these shelves. You can clean them out, and you can rearrange them," he said as he pointed to a shelf that had two cans of tomatoes on it.

"Well, Mr. Anderson, there are just two cans of tomatoes!"

I guess it was the way I said "*just* two cans..." that got to him. He grabbed me by the shoulder and said, "Lemme tell you somethin' about those two cans of tomatoes, boy! First of all, it started out with a case, and that's 24 cans. We sold 22, which means we've got all of our money back. Those two cans represent profit, and profit is what enables us to stay open, and that's the way you get your salary. Now, what do you think of those two cans of tomatoes?"

"Mr. Anderson, those are the two most beautiful cans of tomatoes I have ever seen in my life! I mean, they are absolutely gorgeous!"

As a small boy, I learned a very important lesson about what economics and profit really mean. It meant my job; that's what it meant. In the fast-food restaurants, you learn a great deal about courtesy and human relations. You learn a whole lot about teamwork, and the importance of being committed. When you say you're going to be there, the rest of the team is counting on you being there.

You also might be surprised at how much some of these young people make. I've seen 22- and 23-year-olds managing places that do a million dollars' worth of business a year, and you know what? They're making fifty and sixty thousand dollars a year! Now, that was a lot of money in the 1990s! Several of those establishments give the managers an automobile. One of them, for example, a Lincoln Continental; another one gives a small Mercedes that they can win as managers. Take a sixteen-year-old and put him in a place like that, and the managers who are just seven or eight years older with that kind of success—I'm here to tell you that it is effective!

They learn goal setting working in fast-food restaurants, and as a part of being there, they are depending on themselves to get things done. That is so much more important than just working a job. I wonder how many of those young people this will keep out of drugs and crime. Surely those people who are ridiculing them don't think it'd be a better idea for them to get into prostitution or drugs or crime or something of that nature.

A lot of businesspeople go into fast-food restaurants. How many times has an effective clerk been given a better, bigger, or different opportunity, depending on how you view it, just because they were especially nice or kind or thoughtful to the individual who had just come into that store?

As I mentioned earlier, one of the reasons immigrants are four times as likely to become millionaires in America as are the native-born is because immigrants take a job and make an opportunity out of it. Too many native-borns take an opportunity and make a job out of it. The attitude really does make a difference.

There are a lot of part-time jobs. You can start in lawn care. I remember when we first moved to Dallas, our yard man was an African American fellow named David Smith. David only finished

It's not where you start that is important, it's where you go!

about the seventh grade initially. Then, he went back to school years later and graduated from high school at age 24. He started out just cutting yards; then, he started studying how to care for lawns and how to do all the things that go into landscaping. He put his three daughters through university. Two of them ended up as teachers because he started where he could start and then developed it and took it from there.

Moving up from a janitorial job to corporate maintenance happens very, very frequently. We had a lady from Chicago come through *Born to Win* several years ago. She was a beauty queen, but the only job she could get starting out was in janitorial maintenance. She ended up with her own company three years later, with over 100 employees working for her. It's not where you start that is the important thing; it's where you go!

A youngster might start out as a babysitter and decide they are going to have a professional babysitter service. House cleaning can also develop into exactly the same thing.

What it Takes to Be Successful

In our society today, so many people are having to start over. As I have stressed, job security is pretty much a thing of the past. But employment security is absolutely the greatest it's ever been, at least for certain people who believe certain things or take certain steps. But when disaster strikes, and it does strike, how do you handle that disaster?

Several years ago, I watched disaster strike for a good friend of mine over in Atlanta, Georgia. He was worth several million dollars one day, and a few days later, he wasn't worth a penny. I mean, it had all been wiped out! We were talking about it, and I asked, "Well, how do you feel?"

"Well," he said, "Zig, I'm not exactly on cloud nine, jumpin' up and down with excitement, 'Man! Oh boy! I've lost all of my money! Now I can start all over!' But I will tell you this—I made a very foolish mistake that led to the loss of my money. But I know a whole lot more now than I did when I first got started. The principles I've used to get there will take me right back again. It's no big deal. I'm simply going to do the same thing again." And he did. It's his attitude.

What does it take to be successful? Let me share this with you. It's a story which I believe represents what I call *the American dream*. I'm going to talk about one individual and his company a little bit. The main reason I tell this particular story is because I believe it will give every person reading this book a considerable amount of hope—and hope is the ingredient I have to sell. *If there's hope in the future, there is power in the present.*

This particular individual's name is Dave Longaberger. It took David two years to get out of the first grade. It took him three years to get out of the fifth grade. He was twenty years old when he finished high school and functioning at the eighth-grade level. Incidentally, he had epilepsy, and he stuttered. Now, you look at that profile and tell me, what are his chances in life? In the early 1990s, his company did in excess of two hundred million dollars' worth of business, and they projected over a billion-dollar yearly business in the year 2000. How did he get there? What happened along the way?

Let's do a little exploring. When he was seven years old, he went to work in a grocery store. As a seven-year-old, he learned something that if each one of us will learn, it'll be helpful in our careers. He learned that the best way to keep the boss off his back was to anticipate what the boss wanted and do it before the boss had to tell him. Doesn't that give him employment security right there? What did he do as a child? He started shoveling snow, mowing grass, delivering papers, and hauling trash.

Interestingly enough, his family started calling him "the twenty-five-cent millionaire." Isn't it ironic, sometimes, how when you hang a label on somebody like that it does take place?

He was a student of life. See, most of the time we miss some of the obvious. The truth of the matter is, most of us miss a lot of the things that go on in life. Dave Longaberger was not a brilliant student in school, but he was a brilliant student in life. Early on, he started learning by observing things. For example, with fourteen children in the family, they only had one bathroom. One of his early goals was to have his own bathroom.

He learned to set goals early on. He discovered that if he worked in a certain way and did certain things, he had a better chance to get the things he wanted. For example, when he opened his restaurant; when he sold Fuller brushes, when he did anything, really, he always thought in terms of *my customers*, not the companies. He knew if he treated his customers properly, he had a chance to improve himself and thus improve his business.

One thing he learned was this: All jobs have similarities, and that is they all involve people skills. It doesn't make any difference what the job is; it is a person-to-person thing. He also learned that any job could be fun. He discovered that the more he enjoyed his work and demonstrated that he enjoyed the work, the more fun the customers had and the more the customers bought from him. He learned from everybody and everywhere that he went. He was in the Army for a spell, and he learned the advantages of uniformity, control and consistency, and the advantages of having a central headquarters. He went to graduate school in life. Basically, he was a risk-taker. There's risk in everything we do. He scraped up a few dollars to open a little restaurant in Dresden, Ohio (he'd already had a little grocery store). When he got ready to open his restaurant, he had $135 in cash left. He bought $135 worth of food to serve breakfast with. When he had sold breakfast, he went back to the store and bought the food for lunch. When he finished lunch, he bought more food for the dinner. And that's the way it got started.

His family had been in the basket-making business years earlier. His dad had quit making them, except for a rare few every once in a while. In 1965 he decided he wanted to reopen the business. Every member of his family said, "Dave, you can't do that!" They tried to discourage him. But he'd been looking at imported baskets, and they weren't of the same quality they had been making, so he decided he was going to get back in the business.

Was it always spectacularly successful? No way! In 1986, they owed over five and a half million dollars—not counting the IRS bill, in which case they owed a million and a half dollars. There were about 5,000 people involved. Most of them were the people who distributed and made baskets and worked for him. With all that debt, he went to them and said, "As you know, I've always been up-front, straightforward, and told you the truth. This business is going to make it. I'm going to ask you to trust me, and in some way or other, we will pay the bill." Because his word had always been his bond, everybody stayed with him.

What does he do that is different? He makes every person feel important. Every basket that they produce carries the signature of the person who made it. Dave Longaberger makes every individual know that they are unique. He has a unique management style, too. He doesn't have the supervisors evaluating the workers; he has the workers evaluating the supervisors. When those evaluations come in, he knows what he has to do.

Dave Longaberger is a people-person, almost to an extreme. He says that if you take care of your people, they're going to take care of you. If you let them shine and make them feel important, they'll want to come to work. Then it becomes not just a job; it is a family of people. Their perspective is always solid. He uses common sense in virtually everything. The Golden Rule is the principle upon which they operate, and he says competition's the best thing that ever happened to him, because your competition will point out your weaknesses. They will teach you things. Think of all the lessons we're discovering here in just one example. They are the best source of information.

Remember, when he graduated from high school at age twenty, he was reading at the eighth-grade level. But what happened to him that was so life-changing? What set him apart? He learned to appreciate his own uniqueness; that he was different than the rest. He knew he loved people. He respected people. He got along with people. So, he started using the things that he *did* have.

He also believed that every company should put something back into the community in which it is living. For example, in Dresden, Ohio, you will find one of the neatest, cleanest cities that you will ever come across. It's a small place, but they pay for cutting the grass up and down Main Street because that attracts visitors. Now, the fact that they have a nice factory and great restaurants gave Dave a reason for doing so, but he is the one who initiated that action. He truly has an over-the-top attitude. I like to use these phrases: He moved his company from survival to stability from the time they had gotten so deeply in debt; from stability to success, and from success to significance. See, I believe that's what life really has to offer.

I've got a couple of good friends who lived down in south Alabama years ago. Their names were Bernard Haygood and Jimmy Glenn. One day, they were out riding through the south Alabama foothills. It was a hot August day, and as they were riding along, they got awfully thirsty and saw this old abandoned farmhouse. Bernard was driving, so he pulled in behind the farmhouse and looked over; sure enough, there was an old pump. He hopped out of the car and ran over and he grabbed the handle of that pump, and he started to pump. He'd been pumping a few minutes before he said, "You know, Jimmy, you better get that old bucket over there and dip some water out of the creek. We're gonna have to prime this pump a little bit." To prime the pump simply means you have to put something in before you can expect to get anything out of the pump itself.

That's really one of the stories of life, isn't it? So many people stand in front of the stove of life, and they say, "Now, stove, you gimme some heat! Then I'll put the wood in ya'!" So many times, the employee goes to the employer and says, "Gimme a raise, and then I'll start comin' to work on time." "Gimme a raise and then I'll start doin' whatch'a been paying me to do." So many times, the student goes to the teacher and says, "Teacher, if I flunk this course, my momma's gonna skin me alive! Gimme a passing grade this quarter, and I'll guarantee ya' next go 'round I will really study!" What they're really saying is, "Reward me, and then I'll perform." But that is not the way life works.

Can't you just imagine an old farmer saying, "Lord, it's true I didn't plant a thing this year, but if you'll give me a big crop, Lord, next year I'll plant more than anybody in this whole county, I absolutely guarantee ya'!" That is not the way you work. First of all, you gotta put something in before you can honestly expect to get something out.

Well, it was August, it was hot, and ol' Bernard was working up a real sweat, pumping away, and finally, he said, "You know, Jimmy, I just don't believe there's any water down there."

"Uh uh, Bernard. This is south Alabama! And in south Alabama the wells are deep, and we're glad they are because the deeper the well, the cooler, the cleaner, the sweeter, the purer, the better tastin' the water."

Ol' Bernard was working, and he was sweating more and more. Finally, he just threw up his hands, and he said, "Jimmy, there just ain't any water down there!"

"Don't stop, Bernard! Don't stop! Don't stop! If you do, the water goes all the way back down, and then you gonna have to start all over!"

We'll never know how much good work is lost because somebody doesn't do just a little bit more. One thing we do know is that if we pump long enough and hard enough and enthusiastically enough, that eventually the effort is going to be followed with a reward, and the water will start to flow. Once that water starts to flow, all you need is a little good, steady effort and you'll be getting rewards that are absolutely unbelievable.

Have you ever noticed this? When things are bad, they get worse. When they're good, they get lots better. It has nothing whatsoever to do with what's going on out there; it has everything to do with what's going on right here. You know what I love about this story? I love the story of the pump because it's the story of life. It has nothing to do with your age or education; nothing to do with whether you're black or white; nothing to do with whether you're male or female, old or young; nothing to do with whether you're an introvert, extrovert, educated, or uneducated. It has everything to do with your God-given right as free people to work as long as you wish, as hard as you wish, and as enthusiastically as you wish to get the things out of life that you really do want.

One of the basic problems is that an awful lot of people, when they tackle a new project, say, "Well, I'll just give it a little try. I mean, if it works out, that'll be good, and if it doesn't work out, that's OK, too. I mean, nothin' ventured, nothin' gained." Well, let me tell you something. When you get into something, you need to really go after it until you get that water flowing. Then that steady effort is what's going to make the big difference.

One of the most debilitating things that can ever happen to a talented, educated, capable person is to get a job—like those hamburger flippers we were talking about—that is *beneath them*, and give it a half-hearted effort and then get fired because they're not productive! "What do ya' mean, firin' me? I've got all this education! I can do all of these things!" Very simple: You were not productive. Now, what does that do to the individual? The story of the pump literally is the story of life.

Hear me out, though, this requires a tremendous amount of discipline. We've been talking about that already, haven't we? It requires character, and it requires persistence. Remember, 175 of the CEOs of the Fortune 500 companies are former United States Marines. They teach discipline and commitment in the military.

On March 10, 1981, on a beautiful clear day, a young man named Morris Goodman was flying his airplane. He was an enormously successful life insurance salesman, had been taking care of himself all of his life, and succeeded in everything that he had attempted to do. However, that particular day, something went astray with that airplane. He ended up in a very serious crash.

His spinal cord was crushed. Half the muscles and ligaments in his neck were destroyed. His neck was broken at the first and second vertebrae. His jaw was crushed, as were his larynx and voice box. The nerves in his diaphragm were so badly damaged that it wouldn't work and he couldn't breathe on his own. He was unable to swallow. His bowels, bladder, and kidneys stopped functioning. All the experts said, "The odds on survival are over a million to one," and, "If he does survive, he will simply be a vegetable."

The situation was not good. But Morris Goodman said something that I think is enormously significant. He said, "The doctors were basing their opinions on test results and past cases. I was basing my expectations to fully recover on a will to live and a will to recover." This is a classic concept of optimism and positive thinking, along with a deep belief in the potential within each one of us.

Now, let me say it again. He had succeeded before in everything he had tried. He had been taking care of his body by doing the proper things, eating the right food from a nutritional point of view, exercising, and following a strict regimen all of his life. He was in a position now where the odds were so tremendously high that he would never be able to do anything, and he couldn't communicate with anybody. His sister devised a card system which enabled him to blink his eyes and communicate very effectively with people. He went through a lot of turmoil; a lot of difficulty along the way.

On November 13, 1981, just a few months after they had said he would not live, he walked out of that hospital. Today, he's been bear hunting, deer hunting, travels all over the world speaking, and he's running a camp for underprivileged boys, giving them a chance in life. They made a movie about him, *The Miracle Man*, and I'm delighted to be able to say that the movie says quite a bit about the fact that he was listening to the motivational tapes that I had prepared which he said made a difference. It helped his attitude when things were tough.

You look at the picture of this guy and here's what you find: Number one, from the first day, he visualized himself as walking out of there healthy and hunting. He had the capacity to focus; to zero in on that one goal. He had a tremendous desire and a will to win. He had the discipline, commitment, and persistence that were going to be necessary to succeed.

Persistence, determination and hard work make the difference.

President Coolidge had this to say: "Nothing in the world can take the place of persistence. Talent will not. Nothing is more common than unsuccessful men with talent. Genius will not. Unrewarded genius is almost a proverb. Education will not. The world is full of educated derelicts. Persistence, determination and hard work make the difference."

Total Success

Now, we've talked a lot about what total success is in the game of life. I sometimes fear because I've said so little about money that a lot of people don't think I have an interest in financial success. Absolutely, I do! Anybody who says they're not interested in money will lie about other things, too! Without a shadow of a doubt. But money is just one of the things in life.

I want to tell you something because a lot of people are unaware of this: Millionaires are boring. Less than one percent of all the millionaires in America are involved in athletics, music, television and movies, all combined. Ninety-nine plus percent of them are people just like you and me—people who are reading this book.

The Louis Harris poll of people who earned over $142,000 a year and had a net worth of over a half-million dollars, not including their home, described these successful people as being "unexciting, middle-aged and cautious. They emphasized family values and work ethic. Eighty-three percent of them were married, ninety-six percent of them acquired their net worth through hard work, eighty percent are politically conservative or middle-of-the-road, and they are relatively non-materialistic." In other words, their goals went beyond money. Eighty-five percent said that their major objective was to provide for their family. Only 11 percent rated owning an expensive car as being very high on their totem pole. Prestige and the badge of success don't matter to them nearly as much as family, education, and their business or job. Then they summed it up by saying, "Not much excitement, but lots of happiness." They have a good standard of living, but infinitely more important, they have an excellent quality of life. Persistence, consistency, discipline, and hard work make the difference. Their lives seem to be in balance.

Another study by Thomas J. Stanley in *Medical Economics,* July 20, 1992, showed almost exactly the same thing. "The profile of a wealthy person is this: Hard work, perseverance, and most of all, self-discipline. The average wealthy person has lived all his adult life in the same town. He's been married once and is still married. He lives in a middle-class neighborhood next to people with a fraction of his wealth. He is a compulsive saver and investor, and he's made his money on his own. Eighty percent of America's millionaires are first-generation rich." Sounds like opportunity is still alive and well in our great country.

"Attitude is the greatest difference between millionaires and the rest of us. They skimp on luxuries but are more willing to pay top dollar for good legal and financial advice. The self-made rich develop clear goals for their money."

One of the most exciting bits of correspondence I've ever received was from a young man named Rich Roosen who lived in Northridge, California. He said, "Seven years ago I was strung out on drugs and alcohol. I was completely bankrupt in all areas of my life—financially, physically, spiritually, and emotionally."

Now, I want to emphasize something here as I talk about this young man. You may have heard me talk about people like Mother Teresa and what she's done; about Gloria Hogg, the African-American who was a racist and how applying the philosophy we've been talking about, she came to love people of all colors and persuasion. I've talked about Gerry Arrowood, the dishwasher who went on to become the vice president in charge of sales of a multimillion-dollar cosmetics company. I've talked about Janet McBarron, the nurse who weighed over 200 pounds, smoked two or three packs of cigarettes a day, had been a nurse eight years, went back to school and became a doctor working her way through medical school. Today she has three clinics, her books have sold over a half-million copies, and yet her number one joy in life is to teach the functionally illiterate how to read.

I've talked about Pam Lontos, who was under psychiatric care for five years. Her psychiatrist said she'd never get any better. She was fifty pounds overweight and miserable in her life. She started applying the concepts we're talking about, and less than four years later, she was the vice president in charge of sales for the Disney radio chain, has published a best-selling book, and travels all over the country to speak.

I've talked about Tom Hartman, the man who weighed well over 400 pounds and had all kinds of difficulty to go along with it, and what happened to him when he followed the principles we are talking about. I simply say all these things to let you know that we're not experimenting. We're not talking about a philosophy that might or might not work. We're talking about something here that definitely, absolutely and positively works—if you will work it.

This young man, Rick Roosen, was a high school dropout with no formal education or business experience, but he did have "a burning desire and a willingness to change. I knew for things to change, I had to change, and for things to get better, I had to get better." Boy, I love that! In order to change, he said, "I started going to AA." There's where you find help. You see, one of the interesting concepts is that all the twelve-step programs will not work unless the person who is being treated does something for somebody else. The only way they can stay sober is to share the benefits of sobriety to other people. They are on call. I've had a couple members of my family who were participants in AA; they would get calls at midnight and three o'clock in the morning and get up to be with that person to get them through the crisis. They will tell you a thousand times over that's the only way they were able to beat that alcohol problem.

That was his first step to a better life. He said, "I devel-

> **Make friends with the past in order to focus on the present so you can make your tomorrow what it is capable of being.**

oped some faith in the future and shut the door on the past." Boy, that is so important! You've got to make friends with the past in order to focus on the present so you can make your tomorrow what it is capable of being. Now, the first two years he got on this program he drove an old 1967 Dodge Dart, rented a house, and then sub-rented some of the rooms just to make the rent each month. He said he was patient—it's tough getting started, but as he continued to go to the meetings and started listening to the health aspect of getting success in life, he went from over 200 pounds down to 163. He's now 32 years old, and he says he's in the best shape of his life.

He said, "I started reading the affirmations. I have been reading the affirmations in the morning and before bed for over six years, and it's made a dramatic difference in my life. I am always telling people I'm 'feeling super-good, but I'm getting better!' I always like to emphasize that they might not get anything out of it, but it makes me feel good in the very process of saying this. My belief system completely changed." He went from thinking he wasn't worth $500 a week to believing he was worth over $25,000 a week. He bought the idea that you can have what you want if you'll help enough other people get what they want. Last year, he earned in excess of $300,000.

He lives in a home worth over $750,000; he wears nice clothes; you know, all the things that everybody says they really want. But then he summed it up by saying, "And the most important thing is I have a wife and two beautiful children. I have more delight in my family than any other phase of my life. My family life is infinitely better than it was. I wake up and I look forward to what I'm going to do that day. I love my life. I love the people around me." He goes ahead to say he came from a dysfunctional family, where generation after generation had known nothing else. Divorce, alcoholism, child abuse—you name it. He changed his direction in every area of life, physically, mentally, spiritually, and he has changed completely.

Why do I say that? If you don't like who you are and where you are, don't sweat it, folks. You're not stuck there. You absolutely can grow. You absolutely can change.

> **If you don't like who you are and where you are, don't sweat it. You can change.**

One Last Look at Success

As we come to the final part of this book, let's take one last look at success. From my perspective, had I made millions and millions and millions of dollars, but in the process destroyed my health and sacrificed my integrity, I would have said, "No deal." I'd be unwilling to give that up in order to have the dollars. I'm absolutely confident that most of you would feel exactly the same way.

I want to say again that so many people still identify success with money. They talk about "the biggest crook in town, that guy lives in the biggest house, drives the biggest cars, takes the most trips," and all those other things. Every time you see one, ask yourself these questions:

How happy are they?
How healthy are they?
How secure are they?
How many friends do they have?
What kind of peace of mind do they have, if any?

How are their family relationships?

Do they have a hope for the future?

Again, you are going to be dead longer than you're going to be alive. You know, the Bible says, "Seek ye first the Kingdom of God and all these things shall be added unto you. For what profiteth a man to gain the whole world and lose his own soul?" The philosophy we're talking about will enable you to go all the way to the top.

When I talk about all the way to the top, this is what I mean: Suppose one day, one of my children says, "You know, Dad, it would have meant everything to me if, when I was a child, I could ever have known you as my dad. Had you ever been there in the mornin' to give me a pep talk when I was going off to school to face a tough test, or a bully, or trouble with my boyfriend. Dad, it would have meant so much had you been there at night to hug away some of my hurts and kiss away some of my tears. Give me some of the advice you've given people all over the world. Had that happened, maybe my life would not have turned out to be the disaster it has." Had that happened to me, I would be one broken-hearted dad, because, like most parents, I deeply love my children.

I'm so grateful I was able to dedicate my book, *Raising Positive Kids in a Negative World*, to my four as being the most positive kids I know anywhere. I could have added, "and the most morally sound, saved kids I know anywhere." You see, folks, when you analyze it, you'll discover that every great failure in life is a moral failure. Ask Pete Rose. Ask Ivan Boesky. Michael Milken. Ask, if you will, Jimmy Bakker and Jimmy Swaggart. Ask Jim Wright and Gary Hart. Ask the legislators in the states of South Carolina and

Arizona, where by the score they rebelled and turned crooked and were indicted for fraud. In the last 35 years in the State of Texas alone, three of our speakers of the House have been indicted. These were men who had brilliant futures and careers in front of them, but that moral failure was the problem.

I read that in the State of Kentucky, for example, seven legislators, including the speaker of the House, were convicted on charges of bribery, extortion, obstruction of justice, mail fraud, racketeering, and so forth. As a matter of fact, at the time of the writing of this book, there were over 1,400 public officials under federal indictments. It caused one lady in the U.S. House to quip, "Don't tell my mother I'm a politician. She thinks I'm a prostitute." When things get to that degree, we have reason to be concerned! It made somebody ask the question, when they call the roll in the House, should you answer "present" or "not guilty"? It really gives you something to think about!

There is growing concern among Americans about the political situation, and yet there's one thing I got excited about nonetheless. You see, in Kentucky, they recognized something, and they passed a resolution. I'm going to share about a third of it; but this, to me, says that maybe people are now saying, "Hey! We've got to look at our ethics, our values; we've got to see what is going on!"

"This Resolution which adjourned the Special Session of the Kentucky House unanimously passed on the final day of their Special Session is presented below."

"Resolution Adjourning the 1993 Extraordinary Session on Ethics in Remembrance and Honor of Jesus Christ, the Prince of Ethics. Whereas, on September 17, 1796, President George Washington stated, 'Where is the security for property, for

reputation, for life, if the sense of religious obligation desert and let us with caution indulge the supposition that morality can be maintained without religion?"

The resolution goes ahead to quote President John Adams and Thomas Jefferson, who I did not know had written a book called *The Life and Morals of Jesus of Nazareth.* They passed out six thousand copies to people in the House, and three thousand copies to people in the Senate. He goes ahead to quote Benjamin Franklin where he said this: "As to Jesus of Nazareth, I think His system of morals as He left them to us, [are] the best the whole world ever saw or is likely to see." I get excited when people start recognizing that there must be a turn in that direction.

If in my drive for fame and fortune I'd broken the relationship with that beautiful Redhead, who's been my wife for nearly 47 years, I'd be the most broken-hearted man you've ever seen. Why? Because I'll confess that after over 46 years, not only do I deeply love my wife, not only is she by far the most important person on this earth to me, but the truth is, I've just flat out got a crush on that Redhead! Somebody asked me one time, "What do you do for excitement?" I said, "I married it!" I believe that's where the excitement is coming from. For the first time in my life, I'm going to take an entire month off. The Redhead and I will spend much of that time driving from one destination to another, doing the things we want to do as we want to do them. We love to get in the car and drive because there we can talk and be together.

I know some of you young whippersnappers who've only been married 25 or 30 years might not be able to relate to this, but after nearly 47 years, I find my wife to be more beautiful than she was on our wedding day. I'm so grateful that in doing all the things that I've been able to do that she's been at my side for them all. You see, folks, again, when I was 45 years old, I was stone broke and in debt. We'd been married over 27 years before I was ever able to give her anything approaching financial security. Yet, in all of those years, not once do I ever remember her saying even one time, "Honey, if we just had more money. If we had more financial security, it would be so much better!" She would always say, "Tomorrow's gonna be better. You can do it." Then she would say those two things that mean so much to every man and every woman alive— "I love you, and I believe in you."

I cannot begin to tell you what it meant to me to have a cheerleader cheering me on every day of my life and praying for me every night of my life, even as she, at this very moment, is praying for me. I simply want to say that having a person with that kind of backing does make a difference.

You see, the giant Belgian horse on its own can pull eight thousand pounds. Hook him up with another giant Belgian horse, and the team will pull eighteen thousand pounds. Send them off to school, teach them to pull in harmony, and the team will pull over 25,000 pounds.

I want you to start claiming those qualities over and over, with more excitement and more enthusiasm, because the more you claim those qualities, the more you will have them. The more you have them in yourself, the more you'll be able to see them in your wife, if you are married; your employees if you're not, your brothers or your sister or the people you live with. If you see them in yourself, it's easy to see them in others. You treat people exactly like you see them. That value is just so incredibly important.

What's going to happen is this, for those of you who are married: Exactly the same principle applies. As you claim these qualities, you will deal more effectively with every person you're in contact with, and that's what's going to make the difference.

Had I been on trial for my life, had you been my judge and jury, even as you read this book, had you commissioned me and said, "I want you to tell me what you honestly believe I need to know in order for me to reap the most out of life itself." If my life been on trial, I would have said to you the things I have said in this book and the one before it. Since so much of it is wrapped up in a story I told in the first book, I want to conclude by telling you the story again.

When little Ben Hooper was born all those years ago in the foothills of East Tennessee, little boys and girls who had no idea who their daddies were were ostracized. They were treated horribly. By the time the little guy was three years old, the other children would scarcely play with him. Parents were saying insane things like, "What's a boy like that doing playing with our children?" as if the child had anything at all to do with his own birth.

When he was six years old, they put him in the first grade—they did not have kindergarten in those years. They gave him a little desk, and at recess, he would stay at his desk because by then, none of the children would play with him. Saturday was his toughest day of all. His mom would take him down to the little general store to buy supplies for the week. There were always other children and parents there, and invariably one of them would make some caustic comment, "What's a boy like that doin' around here?" Or they would say, "Did you ever figure out who his daddy is?"

When little Ben was twelve years old, a new preacher came to that little church in the foothills of East Tennessee, and almost immediately Ben started hearing people talking about him, about how friendly and warm he was, how non-judgmental he was, how he accepted each person as they were. How, when he would walk into a room, the attitude, the atmosphere, and the spirit would pick up. He just had that charisma that makes the difference.

One Sunday, though he had never been to church a day in his life, little Ben Hooper decided to go. He got there late, and he left early. He did not want to attract any attention at all, but he liked what he heard. He was back there the next Sunday and the next, the next, the next, the next, and the next. On about the sixth or seventh Sunday—he had always been getting there late, he had always been leaving early; he did not want to attract any attention at all—the message was so moving, so encouraging, so powerful and inspiring, it was almost as if there were a sign behind the minister's face that said, "For you, little Ben Hooper of unknown parentage, there is hope for you!"

I remind you again, if there is hope in the future, there is power in the present. Ben got so wrapped up in the message he did not even realize that a number of people had come in and sat down behind him. He forgot all about the time, and suddenly, the church services were over. He stood up, as did everyone else, and started to try to run out, but his passageway was blocked. He was trying to work his way through the crowd when he felt a hand on his shoulder. He turned, looked around, and then looked up. He was looking right into the eyes of the young minister, who asked him a question which had been on the minds of every person there for the last twelve years. "Whose boy are you?" Instantly the church grew deathly quiet. You could hear the proverbial pin

If there is hope in the future, there is power in the present.

drop. Then, slowly, a smile started to spread across the face of the young minister until he broke into a huge grin as he said, "Oh. I know whose boy you are! Why, the family resemblance, it is unmistakable! You are a child of God."

And with that, the young minister swatted him across the rear and said, "That's quite an inheritance you've got there, boy! Now go and see to it that you live up to it."

Many, many years later little Ben Hooper said that was the day he was elected Governor of the State of Tennessee and later re-elected. You see, the picture had changed. He had gone from being a child of unknown heritage to a child of the King. I've got to confess that on July 4, 1972, though I had lost my earthly father when I was five years old, I took God up on His offer and became a child of the Heavenly Father. I confessed Christ as Lord. That's when everything in my life changed. That changes hearts, and when you change hearts, that's what changes lives.

I close with a question and a challenge: Whose boy are you? Whose girl are you? Oh, I know whose child you are! Why, the family resemblance, it is unmistakable! You are a child of the King! That's quite an inheritance you've got there! Now, go! And see to it that you live up to it … because if you do, I'll see YOU, and yes, I really do mean YOU, at the top!

CONCLUSION

As we complete this second book of the **How to Stay Motivated** series, let me encourage you to do this: Read this information over and over. As a matter of fact, read it until you can literally finish the sentences you are about to read. Read until you can tell all these stories, because these stories do carry messages. And what you're doing when you finish the sentence and the story in your mind is indulging in self-talk, and it's the most positive, helpful self-talk of them all. I've had so many people say they've done this for years and it has quite literally changed their life.

I'm going to wind up this book with a story you might already have heard, but the point is so important I want you to hear it again.

The story is told of a father who was being harassed by his little boy, so he took a picture of a map of the world and cut it into a lot of pieces and told his little guy to put it all back together, thinking he was going to have several minutes, maybe an hour, to get caught up on his work. Well, in a matter of minutes, the little guy came back, and he had the picture all complete. His dad looked at him and said, "Son, how on earth did you do that?"

The little guy said, "Well, Dad, I just turned the picture over, and on the other side of the map of the world there was a picture of a man, and when I got the man together, the world was together."

That's what this book is all about—getting your life together. After you do, then your world will come together. You see, you have got to be before you can do, and you've got to do before you can have. I've placed in your hands a set of tools which will enable you to be what you need to be in order to do what you need to do in order to have what you want to have. Buy the ideas, use these tools every day, and follow those instructions. If you do, I'll say it again loud and clear: I'll see you—and yes, I really do mean you—at the top. The **real** top!

ABOUT THE AUTHOR

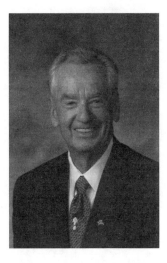

The late Zig Ziglar, a world renowned author and speaker, has an appeal that transcends barriers of age, culture and occupation. From 1970 until 2010, he traveled over five million miles across the world delivering powerful life improvement messages, cultivating the energy of change. Mr. Ziglar wrote over thirty celebrated books on personal growth, leadership, sales, faith, family and success, including *See You at the Top, Raising Positive Kids in a Negative World, Top Performance, Courtship After Marriage, Over The Top*, and *Secrets of Closing the Sale*. Nine titles have been on the best seller lists; his books and audios have been translated into over thirty-eight languages and dialects.

OTHER GREAT BOOKS
BY ZIG ZIGLAR

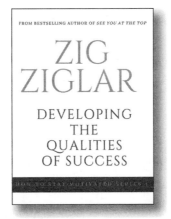